A Parade of Drunks

A Memoir
by Connie May

ONION
RIVER
PRESS

Burlington, Vermont

Onion River Press
89 Church Street
Burlington, VT 05401
info@onionriverpress.com
www.onionriverpress.com

Paperback ISBN: 978-1-957184-86-9
eBook ISBN: 978-1-957184-87-6
The Library of Congress Control Number is available upon request.

Author's Preface

"Every coin has two sides," my mother used to say. In this book, I have tried to convey a shiny side—the social "parade" that swirled around me when I was growing up; but I also wanted to convey the dark side—the dysfunction and the suffering caused by alcohol abuse.

At the end of this book, I list some of the many people who wandered in and out of my childhood home. I have changed some of the people's names, though, because either they are still alive or there are people still alive who knew them. I have also changed some names of businesses for the same reason. I want to be true to my own story and convey my experiences as clearly as I can remember them, but I also want to protect some people's privacy.

- Connie

Chapter 1

The Landscape

"Most children of alcoholics have learned that no one can be trusted." —Abraham J. Twerski, *Addictive Thinking: Understanding Self-Deception*[1]

L ate one night when I was about ten years old, a sound of thumping against my bedroom wall woke me up. A streetlight near a tree outside my window cast long, thin shadows across the ceiling. The noise came again. I went into the hall, opened the door to my parents' adjacent bedroom, turned the corner toward the noise, and saw my father standing half inside my mother's closet, which backed up against my bedroom wall. His legs and backside faced me. He was leaning over, pushing something back into the closet. My mother's legs extended between his feet into the room, and they were moving wildly, brushing the floor. I could see as I moved closer that he was hitting her over the head with what looked like hatboxes and rolled-up magazines. Some of her dresses had fallen from the closet pole, and they lay in folded bunches around her hips. Her ankles and thin, shapely feet moved in and out, and back and forth, and she was making a faint, grunting noise in protest.

On another night after my parents had argued, my mother marched out of the house and headed toward her brother's house, which was about a mile from where we lived. The two of them liked to drink together, and he was her confidante. In the middle of the night, an enormous crash downstairs woke me up. I walked out of my bedroom to the head of the stairs and looked down in the semi-dark. The streetlights outside shone through the glass in our front door and illuminated the bottom of the stairs, where my mother lay on her back, snoring. She had made it up one or two stairs before falling backwards and passing out on the floor. I put a blanket on her and went back to bed. The next morning she acted as if nothing was wrong, and neither one of us ever spoke about the event again.

The road to being drunk is a short trip for some and a long trip for others, but along the way, if people drink in groups, they often have a good time. They feel joyous, exuberant. They bond with their fellow drinkers. Every day, my parents walked along that drinking road—starting at sober, trotting along past the "gay" signpost, progressing to being dark and threatening, and finally arriving at drunk. Most of the time, one of them trotted down the road more quickly than the other one did, so my mother would be gay while my father was threatening, or my father threatening when my mother was drunk. I knew I had better be agreeable and silent when my father was threatening or I would be kicked out of the house. I knew that because it happened to me once, and I lived for three days at a friend's house.

When I was a child, life was full of threats. I was ready to bolt if my father stumbled on the front stoop on his way into the house, or if my mother's mouth was set in a grim line and her face was turning red with rage. My mother sometimes heaved a plate of food at my father that she had been keeping warm for him. Dishes broke and food splattered. I would try to slip away to some corner of the house where people could not find me so easily. And I was lucky that it was a big house. Plenty of places for me to hide—big closets, empty rooms, eaves on the third floor with doors that closed tight behind me.

When my father was sober, he was playful, affectionate, and teasing in a funny way that did not offend, but just barely. After he'd had a few drinks, he became degrading on his way to threatening. My report card full of "A" grades offered him an opportunity to kill two birds with one stone. "Well," he would say, smirking, "at least you don't take after your mother when it comes to school work." When my mother described a winning bridge hand as "impressive," he would retort, "An awfully big word for you, isn't it, Helen?"

My father had a honed sense of the dramatic. He told a joke well, and his timing was impeccable. In a dispute, his first defense was humor, but quick and unexpected anger was another of his tools to help him control his audience. Occasionally, when words were insufficient, he used his fists.

One time when I was about 15, my father began the alcohol-soaked, war-dance shuffle in my direction, his face scrunched in anger and his arm raised up to his shoulder, his fist pointed my way. I was tall for my age. "Don't you dare hit me!" I yelled in fear, "Or I'll hit you back." He must have believed me because, after that, he never physically threatened me again.

I lived in constant dread then, and I have been haunted by fear ever since. When our daughter was fifteen minutes late arriving home from school, I suspected that she had been kidnapped. When my son had a fever, I wondered if he had meningitis. When I am driving around, doing errands, and I'm sitting at a red light, I worry that the truck coming up behind me will keep going and crush the back of my car. My husband grimaces as he bends down to pick up the newspaper on our front porch, and I fear that I have said or done something wrong. I have been told I am an extrovert. When I am in a room of introverts who are comfortable with extended silences, I feel threatened—sure that what I am feeling is not a comfortable comradery but hidden rage. A friend is annoyed and I apologize, because as a child I was given the impression that problems in my family were often my fault and more often my responsibility to rectify.

When I was young, sometimes my father would drink heavily day after day, and at other times, he would drink only in moderate amounts. As he grew older, he drank more consistently and his face swelled and began to look like those pasty white, puffball mushrooms that grew in open fields near our house. Sometimes I would imagine his face exploding in the wind and black spores blowing out of his nose and mouth. By the time he was in his 80s, the folds over his eyes were so extended that they appeared to be shelves below his eyebrows and layers of flesh hung beneath his chin.

My mother was graceful, subtle, and proud when she was sober, but embarrassing and crude when she was drunk. She laughed too loudly and missed her mouth at dinner. She belched in front of guests. She ended up drunk on many nights—slurring her words and heading toward the corner or wall of a room in a sideways shuffle rather than toward the doorway on her way to bed. As she slithered into inebriation, the skin on her face would fold upon itself from the forehead down, as if it wanted to slide off her skull.

Sometimes, she fell into a stupor on the couch in front of the TV. I took it upon myself to try to get her up and help her lurch off to bed, because I knew my father would get angry if he found her there like that. I would start with murmurs and gentle shakes. Then I would move to pokes. Finally, I would plead and prod. I often just had to leave her there to take her chances.

At home, the rules of life that other people seemed to obey—like you can't always get your way, you control your temper, and we are all equal under the law—didn't seem to apply to my parents. They did what they wanted, when they wanted, where they wanted, and to whom they wanted. They didn't pay their bills. They were rude to strangers. They served alcohol to teenagers. They drove cars while drunk (I never knew whether we would get to our destination or whether the car would head into a tree or over a cliff). They screamed at each other and even got into fistfights, which my mother invariably lost. I wasn't surprised when occasionally she had a black eye when she met me at breakfast.

I was taught in elementary school that students don't cheat on exams, and that they must do their homework, be polite to teachers, and get to school on time. I tried to follow the first three expectations, but the last one was difficult. Our house was about a mile and a half from school, and my mother was usually late in dropping me off. One day when I was in first grade, I arrived after a fire alarm had sounded, and the building was completely empty. I hid in the coat closet. About an hour later, the teacher found me there, hiding behind some jackets. When I got a little older, I walked to school whenever weather permitted. It just seemed easier on all of us.

I didn't dare invite any of my classmates to our house because everything was so unpredictable, even in the afternoon hours after school (sherry and beer before lunch and mid-afternoon; formal cocktails by 5:00 p.m.). This meant that I didn't have many friends. Yes, I would be invited over to someone's house now and then, but when I didn't reciprocate with an invitation of my own, these promising friendships ground to a halt. I didn't talk about what was really going on, either. Who would ever believe me? I was just a kid—what did I know?

My two siblings are a decade older than I am, and when I was growing up, they were much more independent. During the school year, they were sent to boarding schools. And in the summers when they were home, they had their own lives to lead and weren't around that much. If I told them what was going on when they weren't at home, I didn't think they would believe me. And I couldn't talk to my teachers or other grown-ups who lived in our neighborhood, because most people in town admired my parents, who appeared to be affluent, were charming in public, and had many friends who were frequent visitors.

"Gracious, elegant, stunning, and classy" were words people often used to describe my mother and father. But I knew better, and as an adult I suspected that many people in town probably knew better, but they held their tongues.

Chapter 2
It's Not My Fault

"An alcoholic is someone who can violate his standards faster than he can lower them." —Robin Williams[2]

We were experts at making up excuses. If the phone rang and the parent who was home was not sober enough to talk coherently, I told people they were both out. If my mother had a black eye or swollen lip, she complained about the loose rug near the corner of the couch. Once when my father was drunk, he missed the top step of the twisting back stairs of our house, tumbled down, and broke his left arm. He wore a cast almost up to his shoulder. We told everyone that he had been injured falling off a horse.

While his arm was in the cast, my mother used to help him bathe himself, but one night they'd had an argument, and she left in a huff and headed to her brother's house. My father asked me to help him. I wrapped his cast in a big plastic bag and stood next to him so he could lean on me—his hand on my arm, his weight against my shoulder—as he descended into the tub. He wore his underpants into the water. I scrubbed his torso, and suds and water cascaded down his back. When I helped him out of the tub, his underpants billowed. That was the first time I had seen that much of a man's body.

My father's injury didn't slow him down. He still drank when he met friends and clients for lunch. He continued to drink starting mid-day and then before, during, and after dinner. Over the years, his drinking followed a relentless, advancing pattern until, as an old man, he split the day into four-hour sections: awake four hours, passed out four hours, awake four hours, passed out four hours. If I were visiting them and woke up in the middle of the night, I would often find him downstairs, reading a book, a glass of whiskey at his side, his pipe in his mouth.

He hid bottles in the back of his closet and in the rear corner of the pantry, behind my mother's collection of shopping bags. We found bottles at the back of the woodpile in the barn, behind the books on the living room shelves, and in one of his boots under the coat rack.

When my mother visited friends for a few days after my brother, sister, and I had moved out of the house, my sister Emily or I would call him every now and then to see how he was doing. For several years, my mother spent the month of February in Florida. One February my father was in such bad shape by the middle of the month that he could hardly talk to us. Then a few days went by when he didn't answer the phone. Emily drove two hours to my parents' house and found him in bed, incoherent and hallucinating. She called for an ambulance to haul him off to the hospital and then to a dry-out center.

He had an arsenal of excuses for his addiction. He once sent me a letter full of them. We'd had a fight about his drinking a few days before. My mother was again away visiting friends for a few weeks, and the family had decided that our father shouldn't be left alone in the house. Emily and I agreed to take turns keeping an eye on him, and I was to spend the first week in my parents' house, after which Emily would take her turn. I moved out of the house the day after I arrived, though, because I found him drinking from a bottle in a paper bag that he'd been hiding behind some books on the shelf in the room he called "the study." It was mid-afternoon.

"I am sorrier than my words can express," he wrote, "that our leave taking yesterday left such a sort of bitter note. You once said to me, 'Dad, do not resort to self-pity.' So please do not think I am doing so. But, I will give you the facts. The doctors tell me my cancer tests are doing well (he had been treated successfully for cancer the summer before), but the pain is still there—three or four times, night and day. My doctor says it will always be there—no worries—but I wake up, take Tylenol or Aspirin and a drink—doctors said OK. Then hopefully back to sleep… Please try to understand… Things will work out and we have much to be thankful for. As Winston Churchill said during the black days of the way—1940—'Look Eastward, the dawn is bright.' Love, Dad. PS. Please tear this letter up."

As you can see, I didn't do as he asked.

Chapter 3
Bravery and Defiance

"Only those who will risk going too far can possibly find out
how far one can go." —T.S. Eliot[3]

My father admired people who had guts. "He has balls," was one of his highest compliments. He seemed physically fearless himself—speeding down the steepest ski slope without a moment's hesitation; steering his canoe down a waterfall on a dare; snowshoeing off into a blizzard, confident that he would find his way home by the cocktail hour.

Some families are hockey families. They pile into station wagons with their hockey sticks and skates and rush off to the rink for early morning practices. Some families are little league fanatics. They attend every game, shouting their support for their uniformed children who seem transformed into adults on the field—warming up for the pitch, guarding the base, catching the ball. We were a equestrian family. My father raised and trained horses. From late spring until mid-fall, members of my family competed at horse shows and trail rides throughout the area. My father was a horse show judge—a position that commanded respect. Horses were his passion, and he would head his mount over the highest jump with a shrug.

The three of us children—my brother Teddy, my sister Emily, and I—were not supposed to feel cautious or show fear. The first time I sat on a horse, I was about five years old. My father plunked me on the animal's back and had the animal walk around him in a wide circle at the end of a lunge line. He was "breaking the horse in," getting the animal used to having weight on its back. I bounced up and down and hung on as best I could. "Use your leg muscles," he said. He had to yell his message, because I was screaming.

A few months before my eighth birthday, my sister Emily and a friend of hers decided to spend the summer giving riding lessons to children in our neighborhood. My sister was 17 and her friend was 15. One afternoon it was my turn to get a lesson. My sister's friend was in charge. My father dropped by the stable yard to suggest that I ride his big horse—to challenge my skills. My parents headed out in their car to meet some friends for drinks as my lesson started. My father waved to me in encouragement out the car window as they headed down our driveway.

The lesson began well as the horse walked around the yard. Then the horse started a slow trot. I bounced up and down, up and down, up and down—and then up and off, landing on my left arm and shattering my elbow. My brother Teddy drove me to the hospital. I don't remember the pain, but I remember looking down at my elbow and seeing how my arm looked kind of crooked. I can still see Teddy's worried look as he turned to glance quickly at me, hunched in the back seat. I spent the next six weeks in traction— my arm hanging above my head, a small rod inserted through my elbow. When they took the rod out to put a cast on my arm, I could look right through the hole to the other side of my arm. The cast stretched from just below my shoulder to above my wrist, and when the cast was removed a few months later, my arm was covered with black hair and was stiff as a post.

A year or so later my father decided I was ready to compete in a few local horse shows. I rode a pony he had raised named Bumblebee. The name was prophetic. She was small, had a fuzzy brown coat, and was willful, independent, and cranky. She didn't like other horses to get too close to her in the horse show ring; when they did, she kicked out at them and bucked, at which point I usually fell off, right in the middle of a walk/trot class. People were supposed to place a red ribbon on a horse's tail when the animal kicked out like that, but my father considered this a sign of a rider's weakness. "Keep control of her better," he told me, "and you won't need the ribbon. Remember, you're the boss."

Well, Bumblebee didn't agree. Once in the middle of a horse show competition, she and I were walking quietly around the ring when she decided her back was itchy. Her front legs buckled as she lowered herself to the ground. I jumped off just in time before she rolled back and forth on her back a few times to scratch herself. When she stood back up, the saddle had slid down and was hanging under her ample belly. People standing around the outside of the ring got a good laugh. My father had been watching the class, and when Bumblebee asserted her independence, he walked away from the ring.

Once, without warning me, he entered me in a beginners' jump class. The first jump was a triangular piece of wood that at its peak rose about 5 or 6 inches above the ground. I thought the class was the usual walk/trot contest. When I realized that I was supposed to head Bumblebee over the jumps, I tried to get out of the ring, but my father stood guard at the exit gate. "Come on," he said, "at least give it a try."

If a horse refuses a jump three times, the rider is disqualified, and a horn sounds to direct the rider and horse out of the ring. I directed Bumblebee to the front of that first jump and kicked her with my heels, hoping she would cooperate. I probably looked as if I were doing the chicken dance with my legs. It wasn't my lucky day. She refused once. Then twice. On my third attempt to get her to jump over the small hurdle, she just stood there and looked at the jump. The disqualification horn blew. I headed toward the exit, but my father was standing outside the gate, blocking the way. "Show her who's boss," he said.

I tried seven more times to get Bumblebee over the top of that chicken coop. Finally, she lost interest in the battle and walked over it with a little hop. Then my father finally opened the gate so I could get out of the ring. I could hear people snickering as I rode away.

When I was twelve I was expected to join my father on a 50-mile, three-day foliage ride held every October and organized by a local Equestrian Club. I had grown too tall for little Bumblebee, much to my relief, so my father borrowed a larger pony from a close friend. I found out years later that the pony belonged to a woman who was his mistress. I met her years later, and like my mother, she was tall, thin, and had a big nose. She was also a skilled equestrian, so she and my father had a lot in common.

Supposedly, this woman's pony was quieter and easier to handle than Bumblebee, but it ended up that the odds were against me. All went well until the last day of the ride. When we were two miles from the barn, the pony took off—racing, racing down the last steep hill toward the finish line and home. Dirt from the road shot up all around me. Trees raced by. I pulled on the reins but the animal ignored me. I clung on for my life. When my father caught up with us at the barn, he was proud that I had not fallen off the pony. I was still shaking.

I was afraid of horses—still am—but I didn't think to tell him I didn't want to ride a horse. My father expected people and animals to bend to his will. Free of the social regulations that bound most people, he could get up in the middle of a meal that had taken hours to prepare and go to bed in a huff if one of us disagreed with him too forcefully. He would ask people to leave the house at a moment's notice if he did not like their political views. Most people didn't try to stop him from doing what he wanted. Fences didn't get in his way (he would cut a wire fence when he wanted to direct his horse into the field beyond).

Once my father was on his way home with a friend at the end of the first day of a three-day horse show. His friend had stabled his horse at the event, so the two men were returning with an empty horse trailer in tow. During the trip, they stopped a few times to "wet their whistles," so the journey took longer than expected. As they reached the entrance to a section of the interstate that was still under construction, they saw a "road closed" sign. My father decided what the hell, he would drive around the barrier and head down the throughway anyway, since the detour was longer and people who had been working on the road would have left for the day. After all, he was expected home for a dinner party, and he was already late.

About a mile down the road, a state trooper was lurking behind a tree, waiting to stop some driver who was bold enough or stupid enough to ignore the "no entry" signs. He pulled his car out and flagged down my father's car. "Don't stop me, officer," my father cried as the trooper came up to the driver's window. "My horse got loose from the trailer and is galloping down the road in front of us." The trooper signaled them on. My father got away with it. He always did.

He was surprised when things didn't go his way. One spring, when the snow was melting but the ground was still semi-frozen, we had an unusual warm spell, and it rained off and on for three days. A brook near our house overflowed, and the road leading to our driveway was covered with rushing water about four feet wide and about one to two feet deep.

My father drove home late that afternoon in his rented Mercedes. He approached the watery spot, stepped out of the car, and studied the situation carefully. Emily and I were on the other side of the stream, wearing high rubber boots and slickers, and trying with shovels to redirect some of the water away from the road. We had an umbrella and an extra pair of boots with us, so our father could park the car on the other side of the watery ditch and wade across. But he had other plans.

He backed the car up and revved the engine. He seemed to expect the car to rush across the ditch. After all, he had decided it would, and he obviously planned to give the automobile plenty of room to build up speed. We waved our arms in the deluge. "Stop, stop," we cried. "The water is too deep," but he was undeterred. He raced the Mercedes forward. It surged into the water and reached the halfway point, leaving behind a path of waves. Then the engine sputtered and died. A neighbor pulled the car out of the water with his tractor. My father was still sitting in the driver's seat, looking slightly puzzled.

His naughtiness was delicious. He wanted people's adoration, and they threw it at him. He invited friends to join him in frivolity or defiance, and they jumped right in. He expected people to believe him, and they did. He did what he wanted, and we all agreed that he should.

When he was in his early 70s, his luck ran out and he was jailed for seven months for a DUI conviction that he had been avoiding for years by convincing the judge that he would quit drinking. The legal community finally lost patience when a policeman pulled his car over and smelled alcohol on his breath. His probation was cancelled and he was off to a jail, or as he called it, "the jug" or "the slammer."

He sent us all letters from his cell, sharing news of his life behind bars. In one letter he wrote to me, he made his incarceration sound a little like a vacation. "All well here, the usual routine at the jug—and I continue to be sufficiently busy at the hospital to make it interesting." In his next letter, he described with some excitement his meeting the governor. "The routine at the hospital was broken yesterday by a Memorial Day celebration—band, flags, speeches. The Governor was there and gave the principal address—reception followed with doughnuts, coffee, and punch. I took the occasion to go up and introduce myself to the Governor and thank her for her gracious reply to my letter, written when I was down in my cell, suggesting my time in jail might be put to more constructive use. She had written to the Head of the Department of Corrections upon receipt of my letter—I don't know whether or not that had anything to do with my getting a volunteer job at the hospital—but in any case she is very attractive and charming."

A driver took him to the nearby Veteran's Hospital and back again several days a week.

My father's mother was still alive at the time (you will meet her in the next chapter), and she turned 85 while he was in jail. The authorities gave my father a 24-hour leave so he could attend her birthday party that he and my mother had been planning for months—an elaborate picnic lunch on the lawn next to our house. My father wore his faded white linen suit, a bowtie, and his white bucks. He had not been outside much in the last several months, so his skin was pasty white. He looked a little like an upright marshmallow. My grandmother never suspected that things were not the same as usual. After all, my father was wearing his usual linen, summer-party outfit, and he was drunk by early afternoon. It was a good thing that he didn't have to return to "the jug" until the following day, after my grandmother had left and he'd had time to sober up.

Inside "the slammer," my father shared his war stories with younger convicts, and they admired his spunk. He told me later that some of the convicts were nearly illiterate, so he gave reading lessons to those who were interested. One of his fellow prisoners—Rodney—was 28 and had been convicted of robbing a gas station in a town in the northern part of the State. My father told Rodney about a poker game that had occurred when he was in the Cavalry. During a gun-practice session for new recruits, one of the recruits shot a poker player "in the ass," as my father said. The poor man was then carried away from the game table, so he had to fold his poker hand. My father then won the pot. My father always laughed raucously when he came to that part of the story. Rodney found my father inspiring. After my father got out of jail, we ran into Rodney in a parking lot in town. The two men embraced.

My father was always attracted to causes that presented him in a good light, as a kind of hero or savior. While he was incarcerated, he spent time planning a development campaign for the prison's library. Always gifted at raising money, he collected $5,000 in donations from his friends "on the outside." When people saw him coming, they took out their checkbooks.

He was good at sales—charming and manipulative—but he had a checkered professional background. When my parents were young, he sold insurance and was successful at it, but World War II interrupted that career. He tried to enlist in an officer-training program in the Cavalry. It was a good spot for him; he was an experienced equestrian and was used to telling people what to do. He told me that his education was not sufficient for the officer's training program, though, so he joined the Army. Lucky for him, he got his way when his entire division was transferred into the Cavalry. Until the Cavalry was dissolved and he was sent to Okinawa, he spent most of his time in the Armed Services in the Midwest, teaching horsemanship to the younger recruits.

After he came home from the war, my maternal grandmother set him up in business by buying a company that made snowshoes and putting him in charge. He wasn't a good manager, though, so the company did not do very well under his leadership. Then he ran the local Equestrian Club. The salary wasn't very high but he was with horses all day long, which he loved; and in this work, he met many out-of-staters (or as we Vermonters called them, "flatlanders")—people with money who were willing to donate to causes my father supported. And he had a cracker-jack Executive Assistant who took care of the administrative aspects of the job.

After that, he became a real estate broker and used many of the relationships he'd built at the Equestrian Club as well as his charm to convince flatlanders that they really needed a second home in Vermont. While he was in jail, we told everyone that he was looking at property throughout the state. He kept his business alive through weekly conversations with his secretary. He even earned a commission when his client purchased one of the properties my father had shown him. His secretary represented him at the closing.

My father was good at putting deals together. He showed people what life was really like in Vermont's horse country by inviting them to our house for dinner, so they could see the glamorous lifestyle that could be theirs if only they would buy that country property. One customer fell in love with two pieces of property and could not decide which one to buy. One had a better house but less land. The other house was too small but the land was beautiful.

"What should I do?" she asked him.

"Buy both," he replied.

And that is just what she did.

Chapter 4
The Matriarch

The one person who seemed able to exert some consistent control over my father was his mother: a round-faced, stocky woman with beefy shoulders and thick ankles whose name was Grace. She visited us for a week every summer and at Christmas. We were never to call her an affectionate term like "Granny" or "Grandma" or "Nana." No, she was "Grandmother," with an emphasized "GRAND"—as in "GRANDmother."

She considered herself a naturalist and studied books on birds and wildflowers so she could instruct us on their various names. I was going over my books a few years ago and found two that had belonged to her. She had given the first one, *A Field Guide to Wildflowers*, to our daughter when she was eight years old. Inside the front cover was an affectionate message: "Given to my beautiful little great-granddaughter, who brought me a bouquet of wildflowers for my 97th birthday." The second book, *A Field Guide to the Birds*, had been given to her by the author, Roger Tory Peterson, who had written inside, "With all best wishes," followed by his signature. My grandmother gave this book to our son. Her message to him was: "Given to my youngest great-grandson, who has great promise as a naturalist, much to my pleasure."

My Grandmother, Grace Brown Maher, is on the far right. By then, she was 34 years old, a widow, and a single parent of a ten-year-old boy: my father.

She was not so gentle and loving with me. I remember going on walks with her alongside open fields. I must have been about seven or eight years old. She always pointed out this flower or that, and told me all their names. On our next walk, she would test me to see if I remembered—a test I almost always, if not always, failed. She would say "Tsk, tsk," and add, "When I was your age, I knew all this information."

She had a prodigious memory. Prepared for the game of Trivial Pursuit before it was invented, she could recite the names of the English royal families going back to the 1400s. She admired King Henry VIII. "Name his six wives. Which ones were beheaded?" she would ask me. She read Shakespeare so she could quote passages. "Who said 'Frailty, thy name is woman'?" she would ask. "What was the play?"

She had a sharp tongue and was smart enough to have some

right to the claim that she knew best. The self-appointed guardian of the English language, she was quick to point out when we made mistakes by saying "bring" instead of "take," or "can" instead of "may," or "who" instead of "whom." When I wanted to tell her something, I became so distracted by her many corrections as I stumbled along telling my story, that I lost interest in completing whatever it was that I had wanted to say.

She liked to write poetry. When GRANDmother was in her late 80s, my sister Emily put together a collection of her poetry as a birthday gift. The poems were lilting and reminiscent of Emily Dickinson's work, but instead of the connections that Emily Dickinson made between her observations of daily life and the profound, Grandmother's works usually focused on herself.

For example:

Dreaming

> "I feel much more elegantly dressed in a caftan
> Than ever I could were I draped in an afghan;
> But neither of these is a boon to the hummock
> That seems to extend from the stern to the stomach.
>
> If only a diet were easy to follow
> I'd turn into an elf, fly like a swallow,
> Or a slender and fashionable lady I'd be,
> And in a bikini I'd swim in the sea.
>
> Ah, me."

To my Great Niece on Her Birthday

> "To be one and twenty
> Do I well remember
> As a time to be happy and gay.
> Summertime in our lives
> Is far from December,
> So here's to a Joyous Birthday!"

To a Friend on Monday Morning

"A lot of silly gibberish
Is hatching in my head.
I felt it strongly coming on
When I first stepped out of bed.
But the theme, I say, is serious
Because it has to do
With food and drinks, and friends and fun
And most of all, with you.
When I step inside your Hall of Fame
I feel a special glow;
It's a gift you have of friendly cheer
You so generously bestow.
Bridge is the order of the day
As hopefully we sit,
Choosing the chairs most carefully
Our anatomies to fit.
This is a game of derring-do,
Of skill, and sometimes more,
As seriously we play the cards,
And hope to watch the score!
Nickels are for rubbers won,
And slams bring out ten cents.
You'd think we play for moon and sun
The mood is so intense.
The foursome at your house last night
Was certainly congenial,
Your drinks were relished with delight,
And your food no less remedial.
Now has come the time to close
This bread-and-butter letter,
With sincere thanks to you again
For making my days better;
And brighter, too, they are
In rain, or in fair weather.
I always feel a special lift
When we four get together."

But to be fair, sometimes she did step away from "me" to a larger point, but I suspect that it stretched her emotional muscles.

Thoughts on Being Eighty-Five

> "When once the shock is over
> It really isn't bad.
> While it's not a bed of clover
> I still am very glad.
>
> That teeth, my own, remain inside
> My head that seems quite clear;
> And hearing aids I have not tried
> So why should I not cheer?
>
> Of course my knees are lame and ache;
> My eyesight's not so hot.
> I'm buxom due to food intake,
> A debutante I'm not.
>
> The truth is I am eighty-five
> With all it takes to make it.
> Yet cheerfully I still will strive
> To play the game, and take it."

Her husband, my grandfather Frank, died of cancer at the age of 34 when Grandmother was only 28 and my father was 4 or 5. Grandmother then worked as an executive secretary to support herself and her young son. My father lived with his maternal grandfather and step-grandmother, and Grandmother visited him on weekends. He told me once that he was very happy living with his grandparents except on weekends, when he had to spend time with his sharp-tongued, critical mother who kept a close eye on him to be sure he grew up with proper manners and an appreciation for the finer things of life.

Grandmother never remarried, because Frank seemed to be the only man who had ever earned her respect. "What did he look like?" I asked her once. "What sort of person was he?" We had only one black and white photograph of him in the house. He was sitting stiffly and already looked weak and sick.

Frank Maher.

I wanted her to tell me that he was six feet tall like my father, and that he had blue eyes, too. Where did he and my grandmother meet? What was his family like? I wanted her to make him come alive.

"He was fastidious," she replied.

I should have recognized that this was high praise, because generally, my grandmother didn't approve of most people. My father never lived up to her expectations. He was not a famous historian. He was not the president of a big corporation. He had not earned a college degree. The only thing he seemed to have done right was to marry a woman with money. And even that was a mixed blessing.

Grandmother valued wealth but she was also frugal. She thought every purchase we made was a "sinful extravagance." Why did my mother spend so much money on clothes? Why did my brother need so many model airplanes? How could my sister wear lipstick when it was so expensive, and why did she need to wear lipstick, anyway, at her tender age? Why did I need yet another cutout doll set? Why did we talk to our friends on the phone so long, when we could write a letter? She was outraged when my mother did not save the egg yolks when she needed only the whites. How could she throw out the cut-off bread crusts when she could make a bread pudding by combining the crusts with the egg yolks that she had unfortunately poured down the drain?

My grandmother was ahead of the rest of us in the environmental movement. Rather than use paper towels, why didn't we continue to hang a long cloth strip on a pole and use it to dry our hands? We should save paper scraps and use them as notepaper. Instead of turning up the heat, we should just put on a second sweater.

As long as I can remember, my father called her every Sunday morning at 10 a.m. He took a shot of scotch first and then popped a few mints into his mouth, in the remote possibility that she had developed an ability to detect odors over the phone line. Grandmother would invariably answer on the first ring, and then we would all gather around the phone to have our turn.

My father was always first and was usually peppered with questions. Had he earned any real estate commissions that week? Had he been invited to the mayor's house for lunch? Would he be visiting her soon? He passed the phone to one of us as quickly as he could. My mother usually hid in the bathroom so she wouldn't have to talk to her.

Grandmother visited my parents several times a year. While she was there my father fortified himself with vodka (he had a theory that people couldn't smell vodka on his breath the way they could smell scotch). My mother once told me that after grandmother visited us, she could hardly look at my father for days without seeing grandmother's expressions pass over his face, and that always made her shudder.

One summer afternoon when Grandmother was visiting, she and my father were sitting on rockers on the front porch when my future husband Jeff and I drove up to the house. My father was crouched down in his chair, his head hanging down to his chest in shame. Grandmother was sitting upright, rocking vigorously. She had discovered his inebriated state.

"Sit up STRAIGHT," she admonished. "Why don't you LOOK

at me when I speak to you? How could you DO this to me?" She paused and pursed her lips. She was disgusted. "You are stupid," she concluded. "Just plain STupid. A stupid, STUPID man."

She had been on her high school debating team, so she knew how to pronounce words to project the sounds. From across the driveway, we could hear that "t" in "stupid" coming out of her mouth like a bullet.

Between her visits to Vermont, Emily, Teddy, and I took turns visiting her. By the time I was a senior in college, she had moved to a small house in Rhode Island that her brother owned and that was near the sea—an easy two-hour drive from my dorm in a Boston suburb. I had use of a battered VW Bug that had belonged to my brother Teddy before he moved to California the year before. Every few months I'd drive down on a Saturday morning, arrive for lunch, suffer through the afternoon and evening, spend the night in her unheated attic guest quarters, and leave the next morning after breakfast.

On one such visit in late October, I kept track of the number of times Grandmother faulted friends and family. She recounted her sister-in-law's problems: "She talks too much. She has little to do except keep house, and she does not do a good job. She does not read the books I suggest." I learned about a great-nephew's weaknesses: "He is not doing too well in school, which isn't surprising. He isn't careful. Last summer when he mowed my lawn, he left big tufts of grass along the edge." She resented a neighbor's dog. "That animal snarled at me, and once he chased a bird away that was enjoying my birdbath." The afternoon crept along. I stopped counting after her 78th complaint.

We had a lot of snow that winter. I was supposed to visit Grandmother on a Saturday in February when a snowstorm arrived. I left early so I would get there on time. It took me over four hours to reach her house. The VW Bug swayed in the wind, and sleet and snow pelted down, making it hard for me to see the road. I had to stop several times to scrape ice off the windshield, and the other drivers made the journey worse. Unlike people like us who lived in Vermont and were used to driving in snowstorms, these drivers tailgated, drove too fast, and tried to pass other cars while on slippery roads. Many cars slid because they didn't have snow tires.

But I arrived safely and only twenty minutes late. I parked the car next to Grandmother's half-plowed driveway, got out, waded through the nearly foot-high snow to her door, and rang the bell. The snow stung my face as I waited.

"What are you doing here?" she asked as she opened the door. "I called and left you a message three hours ago not to come. I've already refrozen the food."

My grandmother loved to eat, and she prided herself on her cooking. "I'm a plain cook," she used to say, "but a good cook." Her baked chicken was never quite cooked enough, though, and the ligaments were usually a little leathery. One of her favorite dishes was meatloaf that she cooked in tomato sauce. When the dish was served, the meat looked like a shrunken, charred island floating on a slick, reflective sea.

Sometimes when she visited us, she insisted on making pancakes "from scratch" as a gift to the family. She liked to improvise—add a little buttermilk or fresh-ground nutmeg—and sometimes we were missing an ingredient or two. One of us would have to go to the market while she got out all the pots and pans she would need. As she prepared the batter, she would usually grumble, "Your mother's bowls are too big. Why does she prefer brown eggs? They're always more expensive." She would finally complete all the preparations, careful step by careful step, and by the time we were eating the soggy result—thick pancakes, with liquid in the middle—it would be nearly noon. All afternoon those pancakes would sit in my stomach like mud.

My grandmother was proud that she was valedictorian of her high school class. I always thought that was no big deal, but years later, I found out that when she graduated from high school, only about 10% of people in this country earned a high school degree. And for a woman to be valedictorian must have been quite an accomplishment.

Grandmother regretted that she had never been to college, but she was a voracious reader and a lively dinner companion—always up-to-date on local and national news. People put up with her because she was witty and an energetic conversationalist. People also put up with her because she was old. Old people seem to be

We finally got out of the building. By that time Grandmother was using two canes to help her walk. She made slow progress as she shifted her weight from cane to cane. When we finally arrived at Emily's car, Grandmother handed me the cane that was in her left hand but kept one cane in her right hand. She positioned herself next to the front passenger seat. Teddy and I stood at her side so we could help her keep her balance as she lifted her left leg up onto the floor of the passenger side while leaning on the cane in her right hand. When she was able to shift some weight onto the floor of the car, the two of us hoisted the rest of her body up into the car. Emily grabbed her hand from inside to help direct the load.

Teddy and I drove to the restaurant in his car, and we all arrived there a few minutes before 11:30. Emily pulled her car up to the deck, and Teddy and I helped Grandmother out of the passenger seat. Then Teddy and I walked next to her toward our reserved table while Emily parked the car. Grandmother shifted her weight from cane to cane as she hobbled across the knobby lawn.

Our three presents lay waiting on the table. My sister had bought her a silk scarf in her favorite colors: wheat, peach, and pale yellow. My brother had found a colorful gift book on English history. I had gathered together a collection of lotions and soaps—all lilac-scented, her favorite. The hand-decorated cake we had ordered was waiting in the cooler air inside the restaurant. Her name, "Grace," had been stenciled on the top with light purple icing. I had tried to get a birthday card from the organization Daughters of the American Revolution to give her but had been unsuccessful. She was proud to have had an ancestor who had fought in the American Revolution. According to my grandmother, we were related to all sorts of historically interesting people including abolitionists and King Henry VIII's Steward (all suggesting a questionably large gene pool).

The table we had chosen was close to the path and near the door to the restroom. The only other people eating outside were a young man and woman, sitting at a table nearby. They were talking softly and holding hands. The remnants of their brunch omelets and toast were being cleared, and a waiter was serving them fresh fruit.

We all smiled in welcome to each other. Before our lunch was served, Grandmother had a rum and tonic and began to regale us with stories from her youth. When we finished eating, Emily went to get her car while Teddy and I began to help Grandmother stand up from her chair. As she walked by the table where the young couple was sitting, one of her canes knocked against the leg of his chair.

"I apologize," she said, "but at my age, sometimes it's hard to get around."

The man smiled at her and responded. "If you don't mind my asking, how old are you?"

She paused before replying. "I am turning 100," she said, holding her head up high, "and my grandchildren have taken me out to lunch."

"Oh, my goodness!" the man exclaimed, shifting his chair so he could look at her more fully. "What was the best decade of your life?"

She thought for a few seconds while Teddy and I stood respectfully by her side. "Well!" she said emphatically, "certainly not THIS one."

Grandmother died in May, one month shy of her 102nd birthday. By that time she was nearly blind and was bedridden. She had decided that enough was enough and had stopped eating solid foods. She lasted nearly two months on liquids alone. One of the nurses who took care of her reported that she said, "I've lived a long time, but I never thought it would take me this long to die."

Grandmother organized a visiting schedule for her family during the final week of her life. My parents saw her on Monday. Emily and her husband were scheduled for Wednesday. She told my brother Teddy and me to show up on Saturday. We drove there from different locations, and I arrived first. When I checked in at the front desk of the complex, I was told that Grandmother had died between 6:30 and 7:00 that morning. The administrator-on-duty had called my parents around 7:30 a.m., but both Teddy and I were on the road by then, and we didn't have cell phones at the time. I went into Grandmother's bedroom to view the body. She was lying on her back; I hardly recognized her because she had gotten so thin. Teddy arrived half an hour later. I was waiting for him in the parking lot so I could give him the sorry news. "You mean, no goodbyes?" he asked, his face drooping. While we were talking, the hearse showed up to pick up her body.

Sitting on the desk in her room was an envelope addressed to the two of us with instructions she had dictated two days before. There was a pile of empty boxes against one wall, waiting for us. We were to pack up and move her possessions out of the retirement home by the end of the day, so her estate would not have to pay for an extra day's occupancy. She had left a list of the things that she owned. Luckily, my husband and I owned a Caravan by then because we had young children, so there was plenty of room in my car for her possessions. What boxes we could not fit into the Caravan would be mailed to our parents.

Teddy and I started by carefully placing her goods in boxes but after about an hour, we just tossed stuff in. We took a final look around her room and noticed a mirror over her bureau. It didn't look like the rest of the furniture in the room, so we figured that it must have been hers and that she had just forgotten to put it on her list. How we could have doubted her, I'll never understand, but it had been a tough morning for both of us, and we just wanted to finish the packing and take the boxes to the car so we could leave.

There was just room for the mirror in the back of the Caravan. It was time to go. Teddy took off first and I followed. As I was heading down the driveway, I looked in my rearview mirror and could see the Administrator on Duty running after us. She was waving her arms and calling out something. I slowed down, figuring that perhaps we had forgotten to sign some papers, but no. The mirror belonged to the retirement home after all, and she was running after me to reclaim it.

There never were any papers to sign after her death. Grandmother had taken care of all the arrangements. She had pre-paid for her own cremation and ordered a plain box rather than a fancy urn for her ashes. A member of her extended family who lived locally was to pick up the ashes at the local undertakers the following week and drive them to my parents' house in Vermont for the service that they would no doubt be organizing in her memory.

Grandmother never left anything to chance, not if she could help it.

My parents held a small memorial service for her in mid-August in their backyard in Vermont. It was a beautiful, sunny day, and about twenty-five people came—our family members and a few other relatives, like my father's second cousin and my mother's sister who lived in Canada. My parents had decided that the ceremony should be a time to celebrate Grandmother's life rather than a time to mourn her death. My mother wore a bright yellow dress with big buttons down the front. My father wore his white linen suit, bowtie, and his white bucks.

Lunch (a buffet of smoked salmon with a green salad) was served after people had had a chance to enjoy a pre-lunch glass of sherry or a beer. Tables had been set up on the lawn so people could feast under the trees. Bottles of cold white wine were positioned on every table, but my father kept sneaking into the kitchen for some celebratory vodka. By the time dessert arrived—freshly cut fruit—he was tipsy.

The ceremony began after coffee was served. Chairs had been set up in a semi-circle at the edge of the lawn. Beyond the fence was a hayfield, where tall, light green grass flowed back and forth in the breeze, waiting to be cut, dried, and gathered into hay bales. Wild flowers grew along the edge, including Black-Eyed Susans—one of Grandmother's favorites. My father gave a short, slurry speech about his mother: how kind, how accepting, how graceful she was—worthy of her name. People looked at the ground, and I heard one mild snicker from the back row: a sound that the person quickly turned into a cough. When my father stopped talking, he shifted his weight and stumbled, nearly falling down. His second cousin Cathy grunted. I looked her way and could see that her mouth was turned down and her eyes were scrunched in disgust.

"Does anyone else have something to say?" my father slurred. After a heavy silence in which most people shifted in their chairs and looked at the ground, my mother's sister stood up and related a story in which Grandmother had been witty at some dinner party. "She was one of the smartest women I knew," she concluded. "I just loved visiting with her." My mother huffed and shifted in her chair.

It was time to spread the ashes. In her will, Grandmother had directed that her ashes be strewn over wildflowers in the field behind our house. In a drunken act of defiance a few days before the ceremony, my father had emptied the ashes into a hole he had dug at the base of a fence post and had then thrown away the plain box that the ashes had been stored in. Emily had dug the ashes back up so they could be spread the way Grandmother had directed. They were in a transparent plastic box and looked a little like loose dirt with small chunks of bone mixed in. My father lurched toward the fence and lifted the box to spread the ashes.

Unfortunately, at that moment, he tripped on a small lump of grass and loosened his hold on the box, which then tipped over. Some of the ashes drifted away on the wind, spreading over the wildflowers beyond the fence, but some also fell in a lump at his feet, turning the toes of his white bucks gray.

For once, Grandmother did not get her way.

Chapter 5

Public? Or Private?

Like his mother, my father had an excellent memory. If given the opportunity, he could quote from some newspaper article he had read six months before. He knew the dates and locations of major Civil War and World War II battles and some of the officers involved. He gathered information about people the way collectors amass paintings or antiques: the name of some man he had met three years earlier, the man's profession, his wife's maiden name, and the source of the family's wealth. He kept track of the names and ages of the children of local people who owned businesses so he could ask for updates when he met these people on the street. People were grateful for my father's attention.

My mother, on the other hand, felt she did not need to remember people's names or details about their lives. It was enough that they remembered her. She had grown up in a family with money, so she could be difficult when other people did not recognize that she deserved the best. If she felt a shopkeeper had been impatient, she would complain in loud tones to the manager. If she thought a waiter had delivered food that was not hot enough, she would take a small bite and then send the plate back with a flourish. If she felt that my father had not treated her in public with respect, she would yell at him in front of friends and guests.

Her wealthy family had taught her early on that she was important—more important than people who didn't have as much money as they had. Until she was sixteen years old, she had her own maid who kept her room clean, ironed her clothes, prepared her baths, helped her with her hair, and packed her bags for family vacations. She never rode in a subway; she considered taxis to be public transportation. In her lifetime, she never earned a penny, yet she was used to buying whatever she wanted on a whim. She accepted an evening at an expensive restaurant as if it were her due.

When my mother was in her early 40's, my father commissioned a local artist to paint a large portrait of her. She is wearing an elegant, black sleeveless dress. A pearl necklace encircles her neck. She is resting one hand on her knee, and there is a matching pearl bracelet around her outstretched wrist. She is bending her head to the side, and her deep brown eyes are looking out into the room. My father hung the painting in our living room and had a small spotlight installed at the top. He used to turn the light on at dusk so the painting would be softly illuminated and became the centerpiece of the room. The portrait is now wrapped in brown paper and has been in our basement for over 20 years.

My mother, Helen Snow, as a young woman.

After my mother died, we received a condolence letter that speaks of her as if she were royalty and that mentions that painting: "About 40 years ago, I remember walking into the living room in your wonderful house... I thought your mother was one of the most beautiful women. And walking into that room, I saw the portrait of her on the wall. I couldn't stop looking at it. I thought that was the most wonderful thing to be so beautiful and also to have a life-size oil painting recording that beauty. In those years, as our families gathered in one place or another through horses, skating, or parties, I loved being near your mother... Throughout all these years I've held her in a kind of reverence, as a handmaiden might hold her queen."

Luckily, the woman who wrote this letter was naturally thin, even as a child. My mother thought that women who were overweight were disgusting. When she saw some woman with a hefty build and generous rear end, she would say, "Look at that," and curl up her nose as if she had just had a whiff of some horrible smell. She was born into a family of stocky women, or as she would sometimes say, "hearty women." My mother had inherited her father's lean, tall build, making it impossible for me to live up to her ideal, since my body type is more usual for our family tree.

My mother wore her wavy, light brown hair in a bun, with curls framing her handsome face. She had a determined look: her brown eyes were wide-set in her face, her chin was square, and her mouth was full. She held herself like a dancer or an athlete: broad shoulders straight, back upright, legs flexed—ready to spring into dramatic motion.

Life presents us with echoes. Some stranger in a store will whip a pen out of his pocket, and I see my husband's hand in the curve of his finger. A harried young mother rushing by with packages under her arm will grab her young son's hand to stop him from tripping, and I remember my own daughter stumbling on the front steps of the apartment building my husband and I lived in when we were first married. Racing out of the house on my way to work, I may glance at myself in the hallway mirror and my mother smiles back at me. I clear my throat, and the sound my mother used to make when she cleared her throat comes out of my mouth.

I once met a middle-aged woman who reminded me of my mother. She was dressed in a lime-green silk dress, and she held her cigarette in an outstretched hand with my mother's extended grace. She pointed her feet when she crossed her ankles, to emphasize her thin legs. She was wearing shoes my mother would have admired:

cut low under the ankles, with green velvet bows over the toes.

My mother had a high sense of style. Dark colors were depressing, she often said; she preferred bright yellow shades and sky blues and sea greens. She never settled for polyester as a substitute for silk. She owned a floor-length silk robe with a tasseled belt. I liked to open her bureau drawer and look at the fabric's soft, orange and yellow designs. When I lifted the material, the floral designs looked like blossoms, fluttering in a light breeze.

My mother had a pair of shoes for nearly every outfit. As a child, I particularly liked the sandals she had bought to go with her off-white bathing suit. Shells in various colors and shapes were glued to the toe straps. After her death, I found the sandals tucked in a corner of her closet. Many of the shells had fallen off, and the plastic toe straps had dried-up and were curled.

My mother filled three bureaus with her golf skirts, tennis dresses, and her many swimming suits. From late summer to early fall, she'd sit in the sun for hours every day, and she liked to wear a different, clean bathing suit each time. That way, if a friend dropped by for a mid-day sherry, my mother would look fresh—ready to receive visitors. By the end of the summer, she was a toasty brown. It is no wonder she had cancerous spots removed from her face later in her life.

She was always ready to dress up for social gatherings. She filled two closets with her short cocktail dresses, longer evening gowns, and floor-length, formal dinner skirts. She also had a long pole installed in the attic, where she stored outfits she had ordered from catalogues: a dark blue wool suit with a matching hat and a water-resistant, light yellow spring coat. On the pole were even a few dresses that had been made for her before and shortly after she got married: a silver flapper dress with sequins and a black velvet gown with a hand-beaded jacket. Her wedding dress also hung there, but by then it was torn here and there, and its silky sheen had darkened with age.

Despite her elegance, my mother seemed to lack confidence in her considerable intelligence. She was a slow reader, and she often grew impatient with books, so over time her bedside table became littered with her rejects. She had not been a successful student. Her parents sent her to an expensive boarding school in England, where she could meet some of the daughters of wealthy European families and find one who had an older brother who would fall head-over-heels in love with her and carry her off into an even wealthier life. But my mother was asked to leave during her first year there. She was glad, she told me, because she hated the place. Only one of four Americans there, she was lonely and homesick from the start.

And she hated the food: overcooked, leathery meat, mushy vegetables, and bacon so rare that it wobbled. But no one was allowed to leave the table until every plate was empty. Peas were on the dinner menu every Wednesday, and my mother hated peas. She said they reminded her of eyes rolling on the plate. For two Wednesdays in a row, all the girls at her table were stuck in their seats until she ate the last pea. Afterwards, she went back to her room and felt sick to her stomach. The third week, she found a solution to her problem. She transferred the peas from her mouth to her napkin, and from there, into her pockets. Once she got outside, she spilled the squashed lumps of vegetables behind some bushes. After a while, the insides of her pockets acquired a permanent green tinge.

The school had an equestrian program, and my mother took riding lessons and flirted openly with the groom. The school authorities were not happy about that, but she didn't care. She was never one to dampen her defiance. For the school, though, this romance was probably the final straw. The Headmistress called my mother's parents and told them to have my mother transported back "across the pond" to the States.

My father always insisted that my mother had been asked to leave the school because she just couldn't keep up with the academic work. "It's no coincidence that the Headmistress sent you home before the final exam period," he said once. Her father had earned his B.A. from Harvard and then gone on to graduate from Harvard Divinity School, and her mother had attended Radcliffe. My mother's academic career was a disappointment in comparison.

My mother's educational history made my father feel better about his own. He was a good student and had graduated from high school at the age of 16, after which Grandmother sent him to a military academy for a year. I imagine that she was probably worried that he was drinking too much, even at that age. Perhaps she hoped that the experience would give him the discipline he needed to abstain. It didn't work, but it did help him get into an Ivy League college on a full scholarship. He did well there academically because of his steel-trap memory, but when he was a sophomore, he got drunk before attending a play at a nearby women's college. He guffawed loudly and yelled insults about the acting in the middle of a dramatic scene. After receiving several warnings, he was finally escorted from the theater. The women's college reported this unpleasant incident to the Dean at my father's college, and my father was suspended. As a consequence, he lost his scholarship.

My mother (in the back, second from the right as you look at the photo), her sister, and her two brothers. Her parents are sitting on the bench.

Grandmother did not have the resources to send him to college without financial assistance. She asked her sister's husband, who held a highly paid and influential job at J.J. Newbury's, if he could help pay my father's college tuition. "No," he said, "but I can give him a job." So at the height of the Depression, my father got a job as a stock boy at a J. J. Newbury's store. People liked him and he was given more responsibility over time. About three or four years later, he was promoted to Assistant Manager in the store on Main Street in the Vermont town where I grew up. My mother's family owned a summer compound at the edge of the town, and she was there for most of the summer. She walked past the store one day and saw my father arranging stock in the display window. Attracted to this handsome young man, she walked into the store to meet him, and in so doing, handed him his future.

They were crazy about each other, right from the start. "Dearest," my father wrote in a letter to her, dated "Monday" in 1935. "Your letter came this morning... It was a swell day and I sat and basked in the sun and smoked my pipe, looked out over the valley, and thought of us and was very happy."

In July, 1936 my parents got married on the family's Vermont compound. My maternal grandfather, a minister, officiated the service. At the time, my father was about to turn 24; my mother had just turned 23 and was already a month pregnant with my brother.

My mother once told me that her parents had discouraged her from marrying my father, because they thought he had a drinking problem. He proved them right at their wedding reception, when he passed out in a chair, my mother told me, leaving her to work the crowd and thank people for their gifts.

Luckily for both of them, my mother's family's money paid for the stage upon which my father could act out his life as a country gentleman, and my mother accepted the job as his stage manager with an organized fervor. Monday mornings were set aside as personal recovery time after orchestrating the weekend festivities. On Monday afternoons, she went food shopping for the rest of the week. Every Tuesday, Mrs. Deller came to clean the house. She worked for our family for over forty years. She was one of the shortest women I knew; when

My parents as newlyweds.

I was thirteen, I stood nearly a head taller than she did. I was sure she never had to pee, like other people, because I never saw her go into one of our three and a half bathrooms, except to clean a sink or toilet.

On Wednesdays in the summer, my mother took a break from organizing and cooking to visit with her best friend Mrs. Borderly, a divorcee and one of my mother's best friends. Mrs. Borderly came to our house that day for lunch. She had white hair and the freckled skin of the redhead that she had once been. Whenever possible, she and my mother had a picnic next to the lake near our house. My mother owned a special picnic basket with a compartment in the middle for her red foam ice bucket and the bacon, lettuce, and tomato sandwiches she had made before Mrs. Borderly arrived. The basket had slots at the side for the bottles of gin and tonic. The two women had a drink or two before they ate, and then they would snooze in the sun.

My mother played bridge on Thursday afternoons with women whose husbands had money. The women met in different houses each week, so each woman was host once a month and in charge of serving a special lunch. The four women convened at our house on the first Thursday of the month. The women drank sherry before lunch. Sometimes my mother would serve cold vegetable soup with sour cream, a salad with spinach and walnuts, or tomatoes stuffed with tuna-fish salad. The women ended the afternoon with cold white wine. If my father came home before the players left, he would grumble about how my mother should be preparing for the weekend ahead instead of playing bridge.

Every Friday morning at 10 a.m., my mother had her hair done at the local beauty shop. She spent the rest of the day preparing for Friday and Saturday nights, when my parents hosted dinner parties and sometimes even had weekend guests. My mother loved parties. She'd cook and freeze casseroles weeks in advance, and her freezer shelves were also filled with dated, labeled plastic containers of frozen, homemade soups—so in a pinch, she could serve meals to a crowd.

My mother once told me that when she got married, she had not known how to cook an egg; by the time I was born, she had morphed into a wonderful cook. When she was old, she gave

Emily and me many of her recipes. Many of her recipes listed alcohol in one form or another as an important ingredient:

Chicken Casserole (serves 6)

Ingredients:
- 6 chicken breasts
- New potatoes
- Parsnips
- Carrots
- Can mushroom soup
- White wine

Take skin off breasts, cut in half and place in shallow casserole. Add salt and pepper and whatever other ingredients you want. Use enough mushroom soup and white wine to cover chicken. Add cut up vegetables. Bake covered 1 hour at 350°F or until done.

Chicken Breasts (serves 6)

Ingredients:
- Three-quarters of a cup of margarine
- Six chicken breasts
- A diced onion
- A diced carrot
- Salt, pepper, and parsley to taste
- One tablespoon cornstarch
- Juice of 1 lemon
- Half a cup of chicken broth
- Half a cup of vermouth
- One cup cream

Cut up margarine and place in casserole dish. Lay chicken breasts in dish. Make sauce by combining diced vegetables, salt and pepper, cornstarch, chicken broth, vermouth, cream and lemon juice. Pour sauce over chicken. Sprinkle with parsley. Cover dish with aluminum foil and bake at 350° until done (about an hour).

Beef with Wine and Sour Cream (serves 6 to 8)

Ingredients:
- Quarter-pound thick sliced bacon
- Six chopped onions
- Two cloves of garlic, chopped
- Three pounds beef stew
- Salt, paper, and parsley to taste
- One teaspoon sugar
- Half a teaspoon of marjoram
- A bay leaf
- One cup white wine
- One pint of sour cream

Cook bacon and remove. Cook onions and garlic in bacon fat. Add meat and brown. Add seasonings and wine. Cover and cook on low for 2 ¼ hours. Stir in sour cream and simmer for 15 minutes. Garnish with bacon. Serve with noodles or potatoes and carrots. If cooking potatoes and carrots with meat, add vegetables to dish one half hour before stew is done.

You can see that people didn't worry so much then about eating red meat, butter, or cream—or about ingesting alcohol morning, noon, and night. Or at least, members of my family and their friends didn't seem to worry. Looking at the situation in a "the cup is half full" kind of way, though, my parents and their guests ate meager meals, because dinner was served late and by that time, most of the people were drunk. That meant that our food supply went a long way; our alcohol supply, however, did not.

Chapter 6
Jubilance

The parties my parents threw were legendary. Their friends and acquaintances lined up to be invited, and sometimes over fifty people attended. A weekend at our house was like summer camp for grown-ups, with group activities, wonderful food, and the requisite cash-free bar. From Friday night to Sunday morning on many weekends from late spring through early fall, our house turned into a B&B with enough beds for seven guests, and if my siblings weren't at home, for eleven guests. And that didn't count the beds in our sleeping porch.

We lived in an old farmhouse that had been added onto over the years and that was located at the edge of my mother's family's summer-vacation compound in Vermont. On the second floor was a sleeping porch that consisted of half-walls of wood and half of screen. The space was big enough to hold a double brass bed at one end and four other single beds along both walls. We didn't have air conditioning and the climate wasn't as hot as it is now, so we would sleep out there most nights in July until mid-August. At night the wind passed through the screens from side to side, and pine branches outside swished back and forth, back and forth. If I read before I went to sleep, insects would thump into the screens on their way to the light.

The sleeping room was located over the living room. My father wanted all the front rooms on the first floor, including, of course, the living room, to be elegant backdrops to his social stage—ready for guests at all times: shiny and on parade. Tabletops were polished to a high sheen. Chairs were placed evenly around the dining room table. Birch logs were always stacked in the living room and dining room fireplaces, even in the summer. We emptied wastepaper baskets every day, and once a week we freshened up flower arrangements.

Some of our rooms were filled with prized antiques from my mother's family: the copper umbrella stand near the front door and the pine table in the foyer. In the living room, books about English history were lined up on the coffee table, and leather-bound novels that my mother had inherited from her parents gathered dust on the bookshelves. Next to the dining room table was a baby grand piano that had chipped ivory keys and that was covered with a shredded Chinese silk shawl. Both the piano and the shawl had belonged to my mother's grandfather.

On top of the piano and on the walls in the first-floor hallway were ancestral portraits. In one of them, my great-grandfather grimaced from atop an elephant, surrounded by servants, all suffering silently in the heat of a long-ago afternoon in India. In another, my mother's aunt was standing on some steps leading to a front porch. She had been a very tall, hefty woman—broad-shouldered and long-armed, 6'4" tall, weighing 240 pounds—unusual for any woman, but in the 19th century, she must have seemed like a giant. In the photograph, she is wearing a lacy, high-necked dress that shines with reflected light. Her husband stands next to her, wearing a flat, dark suit. He seems to be looking straight out at me from the porch's shadow. When I was little, I was puzzled by the fact that his ankles at the bottom of the photograph were located next to his wife's shins. When I got a little older, I realized that he was standing on the step above where she was standing.

My father added possessions he had purchased at local antique shops to the downstairs rooms: the horse-head irons in the living room fireplace and the dining room sideboard with skinny, gold-painted legs that supported a cabinet on each side, where he stored his brandy, cigars, and a wooden box for his poker chips. Framed etchings adorned the walls: red-coated equestrians jumping over stonewalls, racing after a pack of foxhounds along the fields of Ireland, chasing the invisible fox. His equestrian trophies were displayed everywhere. In the dining room, a silver bowl with his name in the middle leaned up against the wall on top of the sideboard, and silver cigarette boxes and cups were scattered on end tables or placed on the front of bookshelves in the living room.

On top of the piano in a silver frame was a photograph of my father in his 30s. He looked tall and sinewy in his Cavalry riding attire: breeches, jacket, and tall leather riding boots. He seemed to have a regal expression on his face, as if accepting adoration from an admiring crowd. Both my parents just naturally seemed to attract attention. They knew how to enjoy themselves, and their enthusiasm spread.

We had to be ready to serve meals to many people, so my parents owned two ovens, two refrigerators, a freezer, and an old-fashioned icebox made of wood with an insulated metal box within and a corked hole at the bottom for draining the melted ice. We kept the icebox in the barn near our house and filled it all summer long with crushed ice, wine, beer, and quinine water for gin and tonics.

My father's round, wooden kegs of beer and hard cider were stored in the back of the basement, where the floor turned to dirt. I liked to go down to fill up the pitchers, because it was cool and damp, and the kegs glistened with moisture.

We were all players in my parents' social game. When young, I was a receptionist and tour guide. I met guests at the door, hung up their coats or jackets, directed them to the living room or to their bedrooms if they

My father Roger in his Cavalry Uniform.

were staying for the weekend, and showed them where to find the whiskey or gin and tonic. When I was a little older, I became adept at preparing drinks. Always ask if a guest wants a slice of lime or lemon in a gin and tonic. Scotch was served in small, squat glasses, and gin and tonic in tall, thin glasses. And someone who drinks bourbon may not be worthy of trust (I never figured that one out, but it was a lesson I learned).

When I was in middle school, I served meals and cleared empty plates. Sometimes I even had to become "chef-in-a-pinch"—ready to heat and serve my mother's casseroles when she was too drunk to do the work. I often got up early on mornings after big parties so I could help clear tables, wash glasses, and dry dishes. By the time I was in high school, I was relieved of my duties except during school vacations and summers because I was sent to boarding school, which probably helped me save my sanity. But during the school vacations, I was very busy at home, helping with the horses and on weekends, wearing many different hats: tour guide, cook, waitress, and cleaning person, depending on the need.

I learned when young to stand up when my elders entered the room. Look the person square in the eyes and shake the person's hand firmly, because a limp handshake was disrespectful and suggested you were a wimp. I was to use people's formal last names when speaking to them, so I'd address a man named "Eddie White-stone" (a made-up name, though it may belong to someone I've never met) as "Mr. Whitestone," and a woman named "Geraldine Butler" (another made-up name) as either "Mrs. Butler" or "Miss Butler," whichever was appropriate. But I was to address many of our usual houseguests—the ones who were around a lot—as "aunt" or "uncle," and then use their first names, whether I was related to them or not.

Uncle James and Aunt Amanda were not related to us but were close family friends. My mother admired Amanda's taste in clothes and liked to have another elegant, stylish woman at our dinner parties. And James was dignified and upright; when he walked, he held his shoulders straight back as if they were wired by a coat hanger. He lent a certain regal quality to any gathering, and he had a deep, rumbling voice and was a terrific singer. Guests often called upon James to sing "When Irish Eyes are Smiling." My father loved this song. He was proud of the fact that he was half-Irish. He even flew the Irish flag from our flagpole, day and night, rain or snow, replacing it only when it was in tatters. When James was not present, my sister Emily took his place by singing "Galway Bay." There was something melancholy, mournful, and homesick about the song that appealed to my father's sense of drama. And the song suggested a loving defiance that was harmonious with his personality.

When my father requested it, my mother would sing her favorite song: "You Took Advantage of Me." She had a rich, deep alto voice, and she would sway back and forth while singing the lyrics.

Uncle Samuel was another frequent visitor to our house. Once a brilliant attorney with a lively practice in New York City, he had diluted his professional life with too much whiskey and found that he had to retire in his 50s to a quieter life with a small office off Main Street in our town. He lived in a small cottage that was near his office and that his family owned. Since the cottage had no central heat, he added insulation and electric heat and settled in there for the rest of his life.

He wore rumpled, seersucker suits and looked upon my father as a close, constant friend. And my father felt that in their conversations, he had at last met an intellectual equal. He admired Samuel, drunk or sober. He used to tell people about the time that Samuel got up from the picnic table down at the lake near our house and said he had to use the outhouse that my father had installed behind a tree. Instead of heading that way, he lurched off in the direction of the water. Before anyone realized what was happening, Samuel was in the lake up to his waist. Another time he left one of our parties to drive home and returned about twenty minutes later, saying someone had stolen his ignition. My father walked back with him to the car, and Samuel got into the back seat, keys in hand. When my father told these stories, he laughed.

Aunt Charlotte was a real relative—my mother's first cousin—and she used to spend a week with us every summer. She drove a black convertible and was a skillful ballroom dancer; she could do the cha cha cha and rumba with effortless ease, and her calf muscles were taut when she walked. She was also a terrific diver. She would walk to the edge of the lake near our house where the ledge dropped

off into about ten feet of water and stand up on her toes to ready
herself. Then she'd leap straight up into the air, curve her body at
the top into an arch, snap her legs back into a straight line, and
head straight into the water, her arms stretched out to lead the way,
slicing the water not two feet from the shore without making much
of a ripple. The first time I saw a Slinky toy head down a staircase, it
reminded me of Aunt Charlotte's diving descent. When she stayed
with us, she would give me diving lessons, patiently sitting on the
grass at the lake's edge as I tried again and again to imitate her grace.
She would also take me in her car with the top down, and the wind
would turn my hair to rumpled straw.

Aunt Charlotte shared delicious details about my mother's early
life. She told me that when my mother was in about 5th grade, she
poured powder all over her grandfather's bathroom in his vacation
home in Vermont because she thought he was a tyrant. He proved
her right when he barred her from the house for a month. When my
mother was a student at the English all-girls boarding school, Aunt
Charlotte told me that she used to sneak out of the dorm at night to
meet one of the grooms. I knew the general story, but she had some
scrumptious details to share. She told me that my mother and the
man had kissed behind the tool shed. My mother was 15 at the time,
and he was 22. My mother had had a much fuller life than I had
imagined, and I was delighted.

Uncle Sherman, my mother's second cousin, was another regular
visitor. He lived a three-hour drive away, but he visited us often. He
presented himself as a country gentleman, wearing knickers and a
tie and jacket, even on warm spring days. He worked hard on his
diction, elongating and rounding his "A's." My "around" became
"ahhhround" when uttered through his lips. He rolled his own
cigarettes, storing his tobacco in a leather pouch and his cigarette
papers in a thin silver case with his initials engraved on the top.
The insides of the first two fingers on his right hand had a yellow,
nicotine tinge.

Uncle Sherman was witty and an excellent dancer—one of
Aunt Charlotte's favorite partners. He was also stylish, much
to my mother's delight. At our dinner parties, he wore his best
tweeds with off-white handkerchiefs nestled in his breast pocket
so that the subtly stitched monogram was visible. And he was a

good cook—another plus at parties. One of his signature dishes was eggs Benedict, which my mother served to her guests for Sunday brunch, along with drinks like Bloody Marys and orange blossoms.

Even Grandmother approved of Sherman because he knew when to say "whom," and spoke sentences like, "Are these they?" He shared her belief that etiquette rules were important in life. When I was about 15, I received my first lesson on how to imbibe after-dinner liqueur from my Uncle Sherman. "Never take too much," he warned, "and always sip it delicately. A lady never gulps." I think back to this conversation now and question why he served liqueur to a 15-year old, but I remember being delighted. I was apprenticing for the family lifestyle.

Sherman took to my family's horsey scene like a duck to water and had all the requisite goods and equipment. When he came to visit, he would unload his handmade riding boots, his saddle, and his silver initialed flask that he would fill with my parents' scotch and then attach it to his saddle. On summer afternoons around 4:00, before the official cocktail hour began, my father and Uncle Sherman would sit outside on the back patio, enjoy a glass of cold beer, and watch our horses on the pasture on the other side of the fence bordering our yard. During one of these chats, the two men decided to treat themselves to a two-week holiday in Ireland—God's horse country. They planned to take their own saddles, in case they had an opportunity to go foxhunting. Rather than check the saddles in as luggage, they were going to carry them onto the plane to be sure that the saddles were not thrown around casually by baggage handlers. They would also wear their riding clothes on the journey, so they would be ready to mount up as soon as they landed.

They arrived at the airport barely an hour before the flight was to take off. The first thing they did was head to the airport's bar. Luckily, the plane was delayed, so they didn't miss their flight. When the passengers were finally called to board, Uncle Sherman and my father were at the "gay" signpost on the road to being drunk. They sauntered to the gate, each with a saddle draped over an arm. I could imagine that their riding britches were puffed out at the sides, and their knee-high riding boots gleamed in the artificial light. Sure, they were deranged—a danger to the other passengers—the man behind the ticket counter at first would not let them board with their saddles. After they agreed to check in their saddles, they were allowed to get onto the plane. Aunt Charlotte told me that once they landed in Dublin, the two men spent the entire two weeks drifting from Irish pub to Irish pub and never rode any horses, much less went foxhunting.

I was surprised and even a little shocked when years later, I saw Uncle Sherman's house after his death. The ceiling in the entrance hall was cracked, and chunks of plaster were scattered on the floor. Coats hung here and there on pegs, their cuffs frayed. Old boots, their leather dried up like ancient skin, were piled on the floor beneath. The living room couch had cigarette holes in it, and ashtrays were filled to the brim with butts. Half of the upstairs rooms were devoid of furniture, and one empty room had holes in the walls. It was not what I had expected, and I felt cheated.

My mother's brother, Uncle Ronald, gave Aunt Charlotte plenty of fuel for gossip. Charlotte could not find out much about his first wife, because he had divorced her years earlier, but we heard that she had a drinking problem—an ironic excuse in my family. His second wife, Anne, died in middle-age. I remember her well; she and my uncle loved to try out recipes together and called each other "Cooks." They would start cooking after breakfast and fortify themselves with sherry or beer while they toiled over steaming pots. Before Anne died, her body from the neck to her waist became bloated, while her legs remained the same and her face was covered with red splotches. She looked a little like a ripe, plump tomato with skinny legs attached.

A year and a half after Anne died, Uncle Ronald wooed my mother's friend Mrs. Borderly and finally won her heart, though it took some effort. Mrs. Borderly was concerned about my uncle's drinking, though he reassured her by lessening his alcoholic intake while they were courting. After the two of them got married, he moved into her house. Unfortunately, Mrs. Borderly predeceased him; he woke up one morning in their double bed and was surprised that she wasn't awake, because she usually got up first. When he took a closer look, he realized she was dead.

He never took a fourth wife—he seemed finished with the romantic life. If the truth were told, he seemed finished with putting much energy into any kind of social exchange. As the years went by, he slipped into a passive, alcoholic fog. When we visited him, he would grunt or sigh to hold up his end of the conversation.

"How are you today, Ronald?" my mother would ask.

"Ah," he would reply, with an exhaling breath.

"We are expecting some guests this weekend, including Charlotte," she would continue. "I'm sure they'd love to see you. We'd love to have you join us. It'll be such great fun." The eternal optimist, she was sure that all he needed was a lively party to be rejuvenated.

Uncle Ronald never did attend one of our parties. He lived another seven or eight quiet years after Mrs. Borderly died, and then he followed her to the grave. My husband Jeff and I got married a year before his death, and my mother was eager to introduce Jeff (or as my parents called him, "Jeffrey") to members of her family. This included Ronald, of course. She thought the two men would hit it off, especially since both were chemists. That Ronald was a chemist was news to me.

The three of us drove together to Ronald's house. By that time, he wasn't able to walk very far. He had a housekeeper who spent half the day at his house, seven days a week. She stayed until after lunch, but before she left, she placed food and drink for his supper on a foldable metal TV-dinner table next to his fireside chair, where he spent most of the day. His brief excursions were limited to trips to the bathroom and to another room on the first floor, to which his bed had been moved.

His housekeeper was expecting us and had left the front door unlocked. Ronald waved to us from his chair. A half-empty jug of red wine sat on the floor at his feet, and a wrapped sandwich sat on the metal table. My mother introduced the two men to each other and then told Ronald with great excitement that he and Jeff had something in common.

"Jeffrey is a chemist," she told her brother. "Like you."

Ronald looked sideways in our direction, took a sip of wine, and grunted.

Jeff decided he would give it a try. He cleared his throat. "I'm an organic chemist. Are you an organic or inorganic chemist?"

Ronald's only reply was to wave his hand toward the wine. His glass was empty.

My mother babbled on about her evening plans. She had friends coming for cocktails to meet Jeffrey, and she had spent that morning with Mrs. Deller, preparing special hors d'oeuvres including salmon slices on toast and watercress sandwiches cut into squares and triangles. She was excited about the guest list and hoped Ronald would join the group or at least make a comment or two about the menu, but he remained silent.

She was disappointed but not ready to give up. "Let's visit again tomorrow," she said to us on the ride home. "Maybe if we arrive earlier in the day, after breakfast, he'll feel more like talking to us." We never did go again, since conversation seemed hopeless.

In the last few months of Ronald's life, my mother called him every day to cheer him up. He would gasp or sigh in reply as she chatted. One afternoon my mother paused in her monologue and realized that Ronald seemed unusually quiet. He had cleared his throat when he'd picked up the receiver so she knew he was there, but after a few minutes she couldn't hear any coughing or grunting from his end of the line. She was worried. Maybe he had fallen out of the chair. Someone had to check on him, and my mother was too upset to go. My father agreed to drive over after he had fed the horses later that afternoon. He found Ronald dead in the chair, the phone receiver in his lap.

The parties went on without him, as always, and guests were not limited to my parents' friends. Like my parents, my brother Teddy also enjoyed being surrounded by people, so he invited his own friends frequently to the house. Nathaniel, Uncle Samuel's only child, was one of Teddy's close friends. Nathaniel and Teddy made an odd pair, because Teddy was well over six feet tall by the time he was eighteen, and Nathaniel never grew to be taller than five foot six inches. In addition, he had the bad luck to be born with an over-active sense of his own importance. No matter what anyone said or did, Nate knew better. It was almost as if Grandmother had taught him a lesson in superiority.

Teddy seemed to be the only person free of the need for Nate's helpful instructions. It wasn't that Teddy was perfect—far from it. He walked into the house with shoes caked with mud. He left his dirty shirts on the floor of his room instead of putting them in the hamper in our bathroom. He drank orange juice directly from the carton, and even if the carton were empty, he would put it back into the refrigerator. He used paper from the kitchen note pad to make paper airplanes without noticing the phone messages written on top. But Nate didn't seem to notice Ted's faults. He became mute when the two of them were together.

I was invited back to my childhood house when I was in my 60s. Maintenance had been neglected after my family had moved away, and the house had been chopped up into five apartments. The new owners were a family: grandparents, their son and his wife, and a granddaughter. The family members were renovating the house and were interested in restoring as much as they could. They had some questions about what doors and windows were original and how the rooms had been used. They also intended to reduce the number of apartments in the house to create a larger single-family unit in the middle to which they planned to add a room to create a smaller, connected in-law apartment.

I stood at the bottom of the stairs leading to the second floor, on the exact spot where my mother had passed out on the floor those many years before. In the kitchen, her dishwasher, cabinets, and counter tops from the 1950s welcomed me. The new family had placed the living room furniture just the way it had been placed when we lived there. The younger couple had taken over my parents' bedroom, and their daughter had the bedroom that led to the sleeping porch, which was now her playroom. (They had window air conditioners so they didn't need to use the space as a sleeping porch.) The closet where my father had hit my mother as she lay on the floor was now a passageway that led to my old bedroom, which was now the walk-in closet for the master bedroom. The third floor bedroom was now a home office. The bathrooms had been redone, and the half bath on the first floor now housed a tub.

The house was different but in many ways was also the same: the stairs I used to climb every day to my bedroom, the eaves in the third-floor hallway where I used to hide when things got violent between my parents, and the kitchen where I used to wash dishes after my parents' big parties. The closet where I hung up guests' coats was still there. I could almost hear echoes of the voices of my parents, siblings, and some of our relatives, including Uncle

Ronald and Aunt Charlotte. The present and the past merged as I walked through the living room and peered into my brother's bedroom, and I was surrounded by ghosts.

Chapter 7

The Gang

Our visitors and guests as well as members of our own family roamed in packs, like dogs. When my friends described their lives in summer camp, moving around with their assigned groups from archery to swimming to hiking, I thought that sounded a lot like life in my house. When I followed my siblings to boarding school, I found it familiar to melt into the field hockey or softball team and commit myself to the greater whole. Some of the other students had to learn the subtleties of group cooperation on the field: that sixth sense that let them know where their teammates were for the pass, the instinct that led them to approach an unguarded opponent, the agreement that it did not matter who made the goal as long as it was someone on their team. I knew all of this already. I understood that the group's needs were more important than my own, and I felt most useful when I was one of many.

We were an athletic family, partly because many sports are group pursuits. Teddy, Emily, and I learned to play tennis when we were young so we could join the game when a fourth was needed for doubles. We formed a softball team with our parents and their friends and challenged a team from a neighboring town for an annual game. We conquered cross-country skiing so we could join the group on winter picnics in the woods and enjoy my mother's homemade picnic soup—heavily laced with alcohol.

Snow Picnic Soup (recipe for one serving)
- Two ounces of vodka
- Four ounces of hot beef bouillon
- Salt and pepper to taste

Mix ingredients, pour into thermos.

The nearby lake was a weekend destination. In the summer, houseguests joined us for picnic lunches, which took up the better part of a day. In the winter, we convened at the lake for ice hockey games. We would pack up food and drinks early in the morning and load the supplies into the family Jeep. Uncle Sherman didn't skate, so when he visited us in the winter, my mother would drive my parents' Jeep down to the lake with Sherman at her side. The two of them would then put the wine and beer bottles in a snow bank to keep them cold, set up portable chairs, and put plastic glasses and paper plates on a picnic table that sat there year round. Uncle Sherman was the one who started a fire, using kindling and logs stored in a small, three-sided shed nearby that my family called "the lean-to." The fire melted the snow beneath and then lowered itself onto the ground. Then the two of them would cook hotdogs and hamburgers for the hungry people who would shortly arrive.

My father and our guests would cross-country ski or snowshoe down to the lake, and by the time they arrived, hamburgers were cooking on a grill positioned over the fire—a grill that my grand-parents had used in that same location. At the end of the day, Sherman would help my mother load up the Jeep with whatever food and drinks were left. Sometimes the ice hockey game lasted so long that it would be nearly dusk by the time the two of them drove the Jeep back to the house.

Once Sherman came into our house hysterical after such a trip. He'd had to take a second trip to the lake to pick up some wine that had been left behind. When he returned, he found my mother in the kitchen, pouring herself a scotch and soda. "My Gawd, Hen," he said, in his loud booming voice (my mother's name was "Helen," but Sherman called her "Hen"), "Roger's passed out in the driveway, and

I didn't see him until I nearly ran over him with the Jeep."

Sometimes before an ice hockey game, the ice had to be plowed. Most winters, a foot or more of snow covered the ice, which when revealed, turned out to be white, bumpy, and cracked. On rare occasions, if the lake had frozen quickly enough, we had "black ice" that was so clear that it appeared to be nearly transparent, except for a few small air bubbles that were suspended here and there in the ice. Looking through the ice's depths, I almost felt as if

My father, cross-country skiing to the lake.

I could see the water plants swaying in the freezing currents down near the bottom.

My father and Teddy took turns plowing the snow off the ice with my great-grandfather's hand-pushed wooden blade, or if the snow was very deep, they used the Jeep and plow. But first someone had to chop a hole in the ice to be sure it was thick enough to support the vehicle's weight. My father thought five inches was thick enough; my mother preferred eight. Once the ice wasn't as evenly thick as my father had thought, and when he drove the Jeep onto the lake's frozen surface, the ice snapped and popped and rolled and heaved. From the shore, we could see the Jeep swaying, and we shouted at him but he could not hear our cries over the engine's growl. He saw us but just waved at us dismissively. When he finally felt the ice's motions beneath the Jeep, he turned the vehicle toward shore and tried to drive to safety. Five feet from the bank, the ice broke beneath the vehicle, and the Jeep began to lurch backward into the water. My father jumped out and barely reached land. The Jeep had to be dragged out of the lake with a chain attached to a bulldozer.

Skiing and skating involved a lot of physical activity, but even in less vigorous activities, we were rarely alone. When we went for a walk, our guests joined us. Our croquet set was set up all summer long, so when friends dropped by we could have an impromptu game. If enough people were spending the weekend in our house, we played parlor games before dinner; Charades was a favorite. We'd split into two groups, separate into two rooms, and think of book titles, song lyrics, or well-known quotes for our opponents to act out to their own team. We knew that if we gave my father the title of a recently released movie, he would use up all the allotted time and weaken his team's score because he never went to the movie theater in town and he hated television. He called it "the boob tube."

Once we assigned him the title of the song in the movie *The Graduate*, "Mrs. Robinson." He pretended he was making a toast to a dignitary. Another time, he had to act out the movie title, *The Seven Year Itch*. He thought it was the name of some rare disease, and he stood in the middle of the room and scratched himself all over.

My father remembered obscure quotes from Shakespeare's sonnets to give to members of his own family. He picked particularly difficult ones for my mother when she was on the opposite team. She would have to ask for his help before acting out her assignment, and the two of them would remove themselves to the kitchen to confer. He would often become impatient with her, and we could hear him raise his voice.

Another game we liked to play—the Dictionary Game—didn't require teams, but it worked well if we had only a few people for dinner—fewer than ten—and they had not had too much to drink. One person would read a complicated word from the dictionary, and we would all make up definitions. The real definition was disguised and thrown into the pile of possibilities, which the person in charge would read aloud, one by one. Then we would all vote on what definition was correct. Whoever guessed the real definition got a point. When it was my turn to play, I would pick weird words like "boulevardier" and "pleonasm"—words I had never heard of. Words that probably few people present had ever heard of. Probably few people in the country had heard of.

Sometimes when things were raucous but not out of control yet, we would organize a game of Sardines, which was like Hide and Seek but when someone found the person hiding, that person would also get into the hiding place. Sometimes there would be eight or ten people stuffed into a closet, with one or two remaining players wandering aimlessly around the house, looking for the rest of the gang.

On the rare occasion, if we had time enough to prepare, we would offer a Treasure Hunt. Emily was especially skilled at setting this up. She would spend days planting clues all over town, and she wrote poems that led each team from one clue to the next. When the time came, we would fill the house with guests from out of town and invite local friends to the event. Each team would follow the trail, clue to clue. Uncle Sherman was a terrific Treasure Hunt player. He knew the streets well, saved clues from past games, and kept careful notes as his team moved along in the chase. People always wanted him on their side.

Bridge was often the game of choice, especially if Grandmother was visiting us, and there were three other people who were brave enough to play with her. Bridge is a game with its own etiquette. After you shuffle the deck, you are supposed to put the cards on your left. Once the play begins, all superfluous conversation is supposed to cease. The dummy is also supposed to remain silent throughout the playing of the hand. Only when the tricks are counted and the score is written down can players discuss the general distribution of the cards or the way the hand had been played. Anyone watching the game is not allowed to talk at any point, and young people present are supposed to ask between hands if players needed to have their drinks refreshed. If any of our guests chatted during the bidding or gave directions to a partner while the hand was in play, he or she was usually not invited back to our bridge table unless there was a desperate need for a fourth player.

My father was a reckless bridge player, often successfully bluffing his opponents when he overbid his hand. Uncle Samuel was my father's favorite partner, because his subtle playing skills helped my father get away with his excesses.

My family also liked to play poker on our felt-covered poker table. Unlike when we played bridge, we could be lively during a poker game: make sarcastic remarks, challenge someone to bet more, and chuckle when we won. My mother was a sophisticated bridge player, but she wasn't very good at poker. She sighed when she had a weak hand, was hesitant in her betting, and folded quickly when faced with a bluff.

My father was born to play poker. He had an uncanny ability to figure out whether people were holding strong hands or were just trying to trick him. He could unsettle even an experienced player and go on to win a big pot that his cards did not deserve. He had a secret, which we all knew: as long as he could force someone out of the game, he felt he was a winner, whether the pot was ultimately his or not. This made him invincible.

A family poker game almost prevented my marriage. At the time, my future husband Jeff and I had been dating for only a few months, but we were beginning to have serious feelings for each other. Before we began to consider a future together, though, I wanted to show him my family. If he was dismayed, well, I figured I would rather find out sooner rather than later, before I got too attached to him.

It was early November when we drove up to the house. The afternoon was cloudy, windy, and cool. The sky was gray and the trees were barren of leaves—their limbs stretching out like naked, arthritic finger bones. As soon as the two of us stepped out of the car, I could see that a ladder was set up against the barn attached to the house. My father walked out of the barn and was holding a spray can of black paint. I prayed that the can was empty and that he was on his way to the trash. But no. I introduced Jeff to my father, who shook his hand briefly and then said, pointing to the barn roof, "Can you climb up there?" he asked Jeff, and handed Jeff the paint. "The weather vane needs a good coating." The vane was creaking in the wind. Jeff was cheerful about it and did as asked, but his patience wore thin several hours later.

The poker table came out after dinner. Jeff asked me if we were playing for money. Thinking he meant literally "with money," I said no, we played with chips. He played with energy and courage, betting high and taking chances on mediocre cards. He only won one hand, but it was an achievement: he had refused to back down when my father bluffed. "You've got balls," my father declared, slapping him on the back. I was delighted.

The game ended and we counted our chips. My father's job was to keep the books, but he only tallied up at the end of the game. It had been a good evening for our family. I was ahead by $3.55, my brother by $2.70, and my sister by $4.55. My mother broke even, which was a win for her, since she usually lost. My father was the big winner: $18.75! We all suddenly realized what my father had known all along: Jeff was the only loser, owing us a total of $29.55.

Jeff was dumbfounded. "I thought you said we weren't playing for money," he hissed at me.

"We don't USE money," I replied. "We use chips. But at the end, we convert to money," which seemed an obvious answer to me. But when I saw his expression, I faltered. The word "chips" barely slid out of my mouth. By the time I got to "money" at the end of the sentence, my voice was a whisper. I remember staring at my hands folded in my lap and feeling worried and ashamed.

Jeff pulled out his wallet and paid everyone. He eventually forgave me, but I didn't hear from him for several weeks after that. He remains convinced to this day that it was a plot to rob him and that he married into a family of con artists.

I tried to warn him. Our guests had to understand that we believed everyone should take risks in the spirit of fun. We committed ourselves fully to the moment: playing poker as if it were our last game on Earth; jumping out on the ice, even if it was a bit thin at the edges. We didn't let a passing thunder and lightning storm ruin our swimming. We experienced life at its greatest and sweetest intensity when we faced danger head-on and triumphed.

Chapter 8
Free Love

Drinking was not the only thing my parents and their friends did in excess. Our weekend parties were precursors to the free-love movement of the 1960s and 70s.

You have already met Aunt Amanda and Uncle James. Aunt Charlotte told me that each of them used to be married to someone else. The two couples attended one of my parents' weekend parties. Aunt Amanda and Uncle James took one look at each other and fell in love. They left their spouses, got married, and then had two children of their own—creating a blended family of seven children: their two plus four from Amanda's first marriage and one from James's.

Unfortunately, Amanda continued to enjoy male attention after she married James. She flirted with male guests at our parties, inviting them to dance and swaying around them on the living room floor in her long skirts and fitted bodices. She would prance around the dining room table after dinner was served and everyone had finished eating, and sometimes would allow my father to pull her down onto his lap. When I brought Jeff to Vermont one weekend shortly after we got married, Amanda and James were invited to join us for dinner so they could meet Jeff. She sat next to him at the dining room table and monopolized him all during dinner, leaning his way so that the tops of her breasts were visible. I thought he looked a little like dinner on a plate—maybe a just-opened clam—with Amanda poised over him, fork poised and knife sharpened.

In her 50s, Amanda was still married to James but had an affair with a man whom she'd met at one of my parents' parties. I never knew the man's formal first name but his nickname was Beetle—maybe because he was short and stocky—about 5'5" or so. Luckily, Amanda was smaller still. Small and delicate. Good cheekbones. Sleek haircut. Beautiful, pearly skin. Expensive wardrobe.

Beetle was rumpled in comparison. He was a little pudgy, had brown hair carelessly chopped, and wore jackets with leather patches on the elbows and loafers without socks. Not a fashion plate, but he was a good dancer and had a playful, jesting sense of humor. He was pleasant, warm, affectionate, and fun to be with. Sometimes when he talked, he just seemed to fill the room because he was so charismatic. I sometimes saw people look surprised when he stood up and they saw how short he was.

He was a good addition to any party. He was also a minister—one without a flock—so after he and my father struck up a close friendship, my father invited him to join his real estate office. That may seem like a strange transition, from a church podium to a realtor's desk, but when you think about it, ministers lead people to God, and my father led rich people from out-of-state who were looking for a vacation home into a privileged country life. Not to be sacrilegious, but country life in Vermont was to be envied and yearned for—kind of like heaven. Still, when I first found out that Beetle was a minister, I was surprised. I thought ministers were somber, sober people who talked in a monotone about doing the right thing, like the minister at the Unitarian Church my family attended twice a year at Christmas and Easter. Beetle was not like that. He didn't lecture people who came to our house and got drunk. In fact, Beetle also enjoyed imbibing, and after downing a few glasses of whiskey, he would tell playful jokes and slap his own thighs when he laughed.

Amanda and James had bought a small vacation property near our house so they could be nearer to my parents and participate in more of our weekend parties. Amanda sometimes came up alone for the weekend—supposedly to take a break from her children and to have some time to herself—but really to spend time with Beetle. One night they went out to dinner in Beetle's car—I believe it was a VW Bug with the engine in back and a metal body only about as thick as a soup can. Beetle might have owned that car because of its name. That would have seemed funny to him, I think.

The night was cool and foggy. It had rained heavily that day, and the dirt road they were traveling on had muddy ruts. Beetle was probably going a little fast. I imagine him laughing about some joke he'd told and pinching Amanda's thigh with delight, using his right hand so he could keep his left hand on the wheel. He may have turned her way to give her a wink. Perhaps the car window was slightly ajar, and her girl-like laughter trickled out into the murky night.

Beetle miscalculated the width of a curve in the road. His car skidded to the side of the road, slipped down a bank, and rolled over into the stream at the bottom of the embankment. Amanda was lucky to escape with some injuries to her face—a blow to her vanity, but not life threatening. Poor Beetle was killed instantly when the car landed with a crunch on the driver's side. People living on the other side of the stream heard the sounds of tires screeching, branches breaking, and the metallic shuddering as the car bounced to a stop. They came running to find Amanda bleeding and weeping, still in the car next to Beetle's body.

When she was admitted to the hospital, Amanda gave my parents' names as local contacts and in so doing handed them the responsibility of telling James the sorry news. That very night, he drove from their permanent home—several hours south—to the hospital to see to his "beloved," as he called her.

Amanda and James stayed together until the end of their lives, but they did not spend as much time with my parents after that. Too much temptation, probably, with all those parties. And I would not blame James if he had lost some trust in my parents. After all, they had known about the affair between Amanda and Beetle for months and had never said anything to him. I wouldn't be surprised if my mother had encouraged the affair. Their love would have appealed to her romantic nature. After all, Amanda had first met James at our house and then met Beetle there. Perhaps my mother imagined that

Beetle was destined to be Amanda's third husband, and Amanda and Beetle could live nearby and come to more parties at our house. Perhaps the situation made my mother feel important, as if she had helped Amanda open a new chapter in her life.

When I turned 16, my father decided that I should have a "sweet 16" party. He didn't think it was a good idea to serve hard liquor to teenagers, even though we had been sneaking the stuff for years, but he did want us to have something fun to drink, so he had two kegs of beer set up in the living room (that didn't stop guests from raiding the hard-liquor cabinet). He told me that any friends I invited would have to stay over at the house rather than drive home after the party ended, in case they drank too much beer. I only invited two friends—a brother and sister who lived about an hour away and were classmates of mine at my school. The brother was older than I and had his driver's license. My father made sure that a few other young people attended—people who were participating in a horse show at the Equestrian Club. My brother also invited a few of his friends who were in their mid-twenties, and some of my parents' friends were there too.

I think about 30 people came. The beer ran out and we switched to wine, scotch, and vodka. (Years later, my friend told me with some pride that he had learned to drink scotch at that party, "and in the right-shaped glass, too.") Dinner consisted of cheese, crackers, and some bean casserole that my mother took out of the freezer and heated up. Around 9:30 p.m., my brother played some records, and we all danced in a big circle around the living room. The only things missing were the fire and simmering cauldron in the middle of our ring.

I found out a few years later that two people who had met at the party had had sex that night in the sleeping porch. I shouldn't have been surprised. My parents made little effort to regulate anyone's sex life. Why should they, when they enjoyed dalliances throughout their marriage?

While my father was in the service in WW II, my mother fell in love with a man who had separated from his wife. The two of them used to meet for intimate weekends, I was told. Since my material grandparents seem to have worried about my father's drinking, they may have approved of my mother's new dalliance.

The affair ended when the man went back to his wife, and my mother moved on to other possibilities. I once caught her in a passionate embrace with one of my father's good friends. It was late, and I was already in bed. I woke up to go to the bathroom. There was a crowd in the house, and the noise from the first floor seemed a constant, loud hum as people walked about, calling to each other from room to room. Glasses clinked and doors opened and closed. The sound of laughter drifted up from the first floor to the dark hallway outside my second-floor bedroom.

As I groped my way to the bathroom, I could see my mother and some man struggling together in the corner near the bathroom door. I thought perhaps they were arguing about something, since I had seen my parents push and shove each other on numerous occasions. I didn't realize what was really going on until I got near enough to see that they were kissing and rubbing against each other in the dark. Their clothes rustled against the wallpaper. My mother turned my way, and her eyes were dazed-looking and her mouth open, with her lower lip drooping down.

Many of the women my father pursued were my mothers' friends, which probably made the chase all that more enticing. One of them, Beverly, had met my father at the Equestrian Club. My father would sometimes stop by her house on his way home from work after he had picked me up from school. He would ask me to wait in the car for a few minutes, which usually turned out to be 45 minutes to an hour. Before he got out of the car, he would look at his reflection in the car's rear-view mirror, lick the index finger of his right hand, and smooth out his left eyebrow, which seemed to have a curl in it. I was used to following the family order of command so until he returned, I would stay in the car or sit on the lawn, reading a book or getting some homework done.

Another one of my father's conquests—Betsy—was Amanda's sister and one of my mother's closest friends. The two women had known each other since they were in their early 30s. Betsy visited us several times a year, and every summer my mother took me to Cape Cod to stay a week in Betsy's vacation house.

It was a magical place. I stayed in the guest room that was attached to the main house but that was accessed through its own door to the exterior. That bedroom seemed to be my own separate little cottage. A flagstone patio separated the two parts of the house, which faced a tidal river. Every summer I spent most of the week reading on the patio or wading in the water, watching horseshoe crabs slink along the sand among the seaweed. In low tide, I liked to dig for quahogs. It was gratifying to pull the clam fork through the sand and hit a lump that I knew was a clam. I threw up the one time I ate one, but my mother and Aunt Betsy loved them. I'd throw the clams into a pail on the shore, and my mother would sometimes come down from the patio with a martini in one hand and a piece of lemon and a knife in the other. She would take a clam out of the pail, open it with the knife, squirt lemon on it, and lift it to her lips.

I was upset when I heard about my father's affair with Betsy—not because one of my parents had been unfaithful; I accepted that as part of life in our household. But I had always loved Aunt Betsy. When she visited us or we visited her, she would seek me out and ask me questions about school and my friends. She seemed genuinely interested in my life. After I found out that she and my father had had an affair, I figured that she had only been interested in me because of him. All the warm memories I had of our time together were tainted.

Age did not seem to diminish my father's belief that he was sexually alluring. When he was in his late 60s, he went riding with a few pals, one of whom had brought along a friend—a younger woman in her late 40s. She trotted her horse alongside my father's horse for a few minutes and made small talk. He mistook this polite exchange for sexual interest and invited her over for lunch the following day, supposedly to meet my mother. But it was a Thursday, my mother's bridge day, and she was at another person's house for the afternoon.

When the woman rang the doorbell, my father opened the door to welcome her in. He was alone and stark naked. I was told that she squealed, ran back to her car, and drove away. I don't blame her. She arrived expecting to meet my mother and enjoy a leisurely lunch but instead was greeted by a sagging naked man with alcohol on his breath.

When my father was in his 80's we found out that in addition to all of these dalliances, he'd had a steady mistress for over 30 years. The woman had been a member of the Equestrian Club, and they had met at one of the Club's riding events. We heard that there was instant electricity between them. I imagined the two of them riding together out into the countryside, tying their horses up at the edge of some field and having trysts in the trees beyond, where people couldn't see them. Every spring, my father supposedly went on a weeklong fishing trip to Maine. He told us that a group of his friends rented a cabin in the deep woods, next to a big lake. "You can't reach me," he always said. "There's no telephone, and we have to fly in by helicopter." To get ready for his annual trip, he packed his car with two or three fishing poles, his bait box, and his knee-high rubber wading books.

Why we all believed him, I will never know, except that everyone did seem to believe him, no matter what he said. And it was a reasonable story. He was a good fisherman and loved the sport. But the truth finally came out. Every year, he and his mistress holed up in a fancy resort up in the northern part of the state. My mother may have suspected, but as far as we knew, she chose to take the higher road and ignore the whole situation.

"Faithful" was not a word in my parents' romantic vocabulary. I imagined a long line of potential lovers—people holding squat glasses of scotch and soda or round crystal wineglasses of ruby red Merlot, waiting in dark hallways for one of my parents to appear. And why not? Once guests entered our home, rules about loyalty, fidelity, sobriety, and just plain common sense were suspended for everyone—especially for the hosts.

Chapter 9

Have a Merry

"The Christmas tree, twinkling with lights, had a mountain of gifts piled up beneath it, like offerings to the great god of excess." —Tess Gerritsen[4]

My mother took months to prepare for Christmas: collecting gift catalogues; freezing casseroles; and knitting sweaters, scarves, and hats to give away as gifts.

She created spectacular sweaters and vests made of thick, Irish wool—sweaters that had complicated designs of ridges and valleys. Even now, more than two decades after her death, I see her handiwork being worn by my siblings and even by my husband. Her sweaters and vests were so well-made that they still look almost brand new.

I can't wear many of the things she knit for me, because she never got my size quite right. She always seemed to underestimate my height and breadth—maybe out of the hope that if she knit something smaller, I might shrink in size and girth. One year she knit a sweater that ended two inches above my waist. The next year she presented me with a vest with armholes much too small. The third year she was determined to get it right. She measured my torso and arms in June before she began to knit her gift from me. Assuming that I would gain weight between June and December, she added length and width to her pattern. When I opened the package and tried the sweater on, the front and back were the right length, but the shoulders bulged out beyond my body. The sleeves were so short that they ended three inches above my wrists. The sweater was light brown and the neck was small. When I put it on, I looked a little as if I were wearing a cardboard box.

Still, I've kept most of what she made for me, including two sweater vests—one yellow and one pink—and a white pullover sweater with an intricate knitting pattern. I store them in plastic bags in our basement and every now and then, I take them out and try some on or refold them more neatly. Sometimes I think I can catch a whiff of my mother's perfume in them. She also knit some clothes for our daughter's Barbie dolls that our granddaughter will inherit; and a small throw blanket that she knit is folded at the foot of our guest bed.

By mid-December every year, it was time to prepare our house for the holidays. My mother spread the Christmas cards that my parents had received on mantles and tabletops. She hung mistletoe above all the doorways, even the one leading to the half-bath under the stairs. Her collection of stuffed Santa Clauses sat on chairs and in corners. One of them had a ring sticking out the back and sang "Jingle Bells" when you pulled at the ring. My mother liked to hold that Santa under her arm and pull the ring so the song would tinkle out.

We ordered wreaths with red bows from the flower shop in town—enough wreaths for all the exterior doors on the first floor, even those facing the backyard. With a spray-on kit and stencils, we covered first-floor windows with frosty snowflakes, snowmen with carrot noses, and Santas with bags of presents. I particularly liked the design of Santa heading into Christmas Eve with his reindeer pulling the sleigh.

Every year we unpacked the crèche that had belonged to my mother's parents and set it up on the dining room table. Little Jesus was made of wax and lay in a small manger made of slivers of light-brown wood that looked like toothpicks. Two of the three wise men were made of wood and had long, curly black hair. The third wise man had broken in half and had been replaced with a plastic substitute that wobbled when you touched it. Mary was in a kneeling position next to the manger. Joseph had been missing for years, and we only had one camel. The barn was a three-sided shed with low walls and a steep roof that looked just like our lean-to down at the lake. From the side, it also looked a little like the chalets that were popping up in our valley to house out-of-state skiers who were descending on us in droves, so it felt right when my mother sprayed the shed with frosty paint and put cotton all around the scene to add a touch of snow. At the edges of this little scene, she placed two or three small, plastic evergreens, with sparkles glued on the sides to look like ice. When I was a little girl, I thought that Jesus had been born in our snowy Vermont.

My grandmother usually arrived a few days before Christmas to keep her eye on my father's drinking and to make sure we used every scrap of food in the house before we went out and bought more. There were many parties in our house over the holidays, and people drank and ate a lot. Grandmother was in a constant state of disapproval, because despite her vigilance, my father spent the holidays every year in a drunken fog. One year in early January when I was 34 and she was 93, she sent me a letter about my father's drinking—a letter that I still have today.

"With liquor flowing freely all around him wherever he goes," she wrote, "and the emotional stress of Christmas, and the confusion, the temptation to drink must be extremely difficult for Roger to control." At this point, she couldn't help but congratulate herself in comparison to her son's behavior. "I can't compare it to smoking, of which I cured myself 13 years ago and am now revolted by smokers, not tempted." Then she switched her focus back to her son. "Drinking is a sociable thing, as well as developing a taste for it, and the release it gives from worry and strain, which I think is its greatest attraction, even if only temporary... It concerns me deeply because of Roger's health. I can only pray he doesn't go off the deep end." I think she was a little late with that wish. Years too late.

Then Grandmother got to the crux of the matter—whom to blame (yes, Grandmother, I used "whom" correctly in this sentence!). She took advantage of the moment to throw a barb at my mother. "It takes a lot of doing to resist escape through liquor when his home life is not what makes for real happiness and congeniality." But to be fair, she did try to strike a more balanced note. "This tragedy in their lives (not just Roger's) is heart-breaking to me," she added, "as I know it is to the rest of the family, but a mother suffers most because she is made that way." Then she ended this passage by reminding me where my loyalties should lie. "As a mother yourself, you know this." I can still hear the firm and slightly scolding tone of her voice, jumping off the page.

A few days before Christmas, it was time for a long-standing family ritual: choosing our Christmas tree. My friends were lucky: their parents went to Haggarty's Christmas Tree Lot in town where trees were bushy on all sides and narrowed to the top in perfect cones. We had to cut our tree in the woods, where many specimens were scraggly or lopsided.

When the afternoon arrived for this important task, Teddy, Emily, and I would don boots, coats, hats, mittens, and scarves, and set out with our father into the deep, unplowed snow, down to the banks of the ice-covered lake, and into the woods at the water's edge. We pulled our family toboggan behind us—the one that had belonged to my mother's grandfather—and put the saw and rope on top. Snow crunched beneath our feet, and the air was frozen into stillness. Fortified before we left the house with a few cups of rum-laden eggnog, our father led the troops forward.

Every year as we slogged through the snow, he told us about the time he had chosen a pine tree for my parents' first Christmas together, and it lost all its leaves before the 25th. "Never pine," he reminded us. "Never pick a pine tree." And of course there was the unspoken rule: never pick a good-looking tree. There was no need for that. Better to leave it in the forest, where it would grow up straight and full.

By the time we hit the first fringe of trees, 30 minutes after we left home, our father was less chatty and in more of a hurry to do the deed so we could get back home to the warm fire and rum-spiced eggnog. He would spot a tree with a double trunk or one that grew at a 90-degree angle. "That's the one," he would declare. One year he found a tree that looked as if someone had carefully shaved off all the growth on one side. "This is perfect. It'll fit nicely in the living room corner." But Teddy, Emily, and I wanted a tree that looked as if it had been waiting for us at Haggarty's.

We would wander around the woods, bickering. One tree was too tall, another too wide. A third had a crooked top. We wore our father down. Finally we'd choose one we could all live with, but before we could cut it down, our father always insisted we stand in front of the tree of choice and sing "Oh Christmas Tree, Oh Christmas Tree." By this time, evening was often fast upon us. The wind would invariably have increased and would be swooping along the surface of the snow, kicking up white clouds of ice. My father would take a swig or two from his monogrammed silver flask for warmth. Then we had to sing the song again, this time in German. "Oh Tannenbaum, Oh Tannenbaum." Our voices rose like squeaks into the frigid air.

It was a long walk home, and the tree made the toboggan heavy. We were lucky each year if we got back home before dark. While we were out in the woods, my mother would unpack all the Christmas decorations and pile the presents in the living room. Then we set up and decorated the tree while my mother played Christmas music on her tape machine and served us all sherry. We hung the lights on first; they were tear-shaped and flickered on-and-off. Then we covered the branches with glass bulbs, strings of bells, china reindeer, tiny belted snowmen, and silver aluminum strips that hung down like icicles. We did the work all at once and in no particular order, so the tree always looked a little deranged by the time we were done— as if Santa had vomited Christmas decorations all over it.

Next came the presents. My mother stuffed her lumpy knitted gifts at the back of the tree. She never seemed to use enough wrapping paper so some would be barely covered. We shoved most boxes under the lower branches and then placed more boxes on the rug in front of the tree. Some of the smaller gifts could be balanced on the tree's branches. By the time the presents were all in place, the pile often extended out into the living room. My grandmother always grumbled about the excess and usually sat in a chair near the fireplace, her face puckered up in disapproval.

We opened the presents on Christmas morning. Before that happy moment, though, we had to endure Christmas Eve dinner. At every family holiday, we ate a specific kind of meat: a leg of lamb for Easter, smoked salmon for July 4th, and turkey, of course, for Thanksgiving. My father had a sweet tooth, and he thought that every meat required a sugary partner: cranberry sauce with turkey, mint jelly with lamb, apple jelly with chicken, sweet chutney with roast beef, applesauce with roast pork, and sliced pineapple with baked ham. One year we ran out of applesauce and served apple jelly with pork. He wasn't having it. He pouted all through the meal and refused to eat his pork, even though he had gone to the trouble to smoke the meat.

My father smoked a lot of the meat we ate. He loved his smoker: a metal cylinder with four squat legs that looked a little like a round-headed, miniature robot with smoke coming out of the top. He would build a wood fire in the bottom compartment and add dried corncobs to add flavor. The meat sat on a rack above. He left the smoker in the middle of our driveway near the front door, so he would not have to go too far to keep the fire going and to check the meat. Our house was old and leaky, so the smell of smoke would drift inside even when we closed the windows. It took him almost an entire day to smoke a piece of ham, bacon, or roast beef to his satisfaction, and when he was done, every piece of meat tasted how I'd imagine charred wood would taste.

Our Christmas Eve meal usually consisted of a smoked ham with nutmeg sprigs stuck in all over the top. My mother also served peas with pearl onions, mashed sweet potatoes with rum, and carrots with butter, sherry, brown sugar, and a little curry. We paid Mrs. Deller to make pies—apple, mincemeat, or strawberry-rhubarb—that we slathered in vanilla ice cream with maple syrup on top. Sometimes we also had heavily sugared stewed prunes served with a hard sauce that contained rum.

After dinner on Christmas Eve, Grandmother would sit at our piano and play Christmas carols. Her stocky body rocked back and forth as she pounded the keys, and her voice boomed out, leading us on. "Oh Holy Night" was her favorite. My father had to be sure we sang "Good King Wenceslaus." He knew the words to many of the carols but he was tone deaf and so sang them in a droning monotone. When particularly moved by the music, he would shuffle back and forth at the edge of the rug and sometimes shed a tear or two. We moved through the songbook as quickly as we could, and by the time we hit the last carol, we were racing with the piano in double-time.

Between songs, my father kept his throat moist with swigs of Irish Mist from a squat glass. At dinner he drank glasses of red wine to celebrate the season, so by the time we were finished singing and eating, he was fairly hammered and would head with a loopy gate toward the stairs leading to the second-floor bedrooms. He would ascend each stair as if it were higher than it was, stumbling when his foot hit the tread. The walls along the stairs were covered with family photographs, and he knocked into them as he hobbled upward. By the time he reached the second-floor hallway, many of the photographs on the stairway wall were askew, as if some mighty wind had dislodged them.

Christmas mornings were the same every year. We started by feeding the dogs and horses, mucking out the horses' stalls, and then eating Grandmother's pancake breakfast. By late morning, we were queasy but ready to begin opening the gifts. My mother had already heated some cider on the stove and had added cinnamon and brandy. She had also prepared a new batch of rum eggnog so we could help ourselves. My father lit the fire and poured himself a beer. Teddy moved my father's brocade chair next to the tree, so as head of the family, my father could pass out the presents one by one. He read each label and then gave the gift to me as the youngest child to deliver to the recipient (when grandchildren came along, they each in turn inherited this duty). As we opened each Christmas gift, we threw the paper into a pile in the middle of the living room. When the pile got high enough, Teddy would get a garbage can and fill it to the brim. One year he tossed some of the paper into the fireplace. The fire expanded with a whoosh and a hum as the creosote in the chimney ignited. The Fire Department responded right away. Firemen wearing big, black rubber boots and dragging hoses rushed into the house, and some of the gift boxes got trampled.

It took us a long time every year to get through the pile of presents, because only one person at a time opened a gift while the rest of us sat back and watched. When Emily received one of my mother's hand-knit sweaters, she put it on for all to see. When my grandmother unwrapped her annual gift of a bottle of rum, we all had a small glass. When my mother opened up a new cookbook one of us had given her, we all listened as she read some of the recipes she had never heard of.

My father usually gave us some of his own books as presents. One year he gave my mother a collection of some of Winston Churchill's more famous speeches. After she had opened the gift, he asked her to pass the book back to him so he could read the inscription he had written inside the front cover: "To my darling wife Helen. May this book teach you some of the beautiful possibilities of the English language, spoken by a true Master." He had scratched out the words my mother had written in the book the year before: "Merry Christmas and love to my husband, Roger." He even read a passage or two from one of the speeches. His voice was deep, and he rounded his As and rolled his Rs. My grandmother was puffed up with pride at his diction, but I found it odd that my parents wrote each other's name in the book. Had they forgotten what their spouses' names were?

When I was a junior in high school, my father's Christmas present to me was his copy of *The Complete Works of William Shakespeare*—1375 pages long, with print so small that I had to use a magnifying glass to read it. On the inside of the front cover, he had written, "To my younger daughter, with high hopes that this book will help you improve the quality of your college application essays."

My father thought novels were lightweight. He liked to read texts about generals who marched off onto the fields of war to find glory. He also shared his mother's passion for Shakespeare. He knew passages from the play *Henry V* by heart, and he would often stand at dinner parties to quote one in particular that he found most rousing:

> "Once more onto the breach, dear friends, once more;
> Or close up the wall with our English dead.
> In peace there's nothing so becomes a man
> As modest stillness and humility;
> But when the blast of war blows in our ears,
> Then imitate the action of the tiger;
> Stiffen the sinews, summon up the blood
> Disguise fair nature with hard-favour'd rage;"

At this point he'd skip to the last few lines, which he felt were particularly rousing:

> "I see you stand like greyhounds in the slips,
> Straining upon the start. The game's afoot:
> Follow your spirit; and upon this charge
> Cry 'God for Harry, England, and Saint George!'"

His voice would rise and fall with the rhythm of the lines, and he would sway back and forth as he spoke. Sometimes he would slap the table for emphasis and point to his guests to be sure he was holding their attention. When he reached the last line, he would invariably weep, so affected was he by the drama of the moment.

But he had a romantic side to him, too. Sometimes when he hadn't had too much to drink, he'd stand up and recite the first stanza of Edgar Allan Poe's poem "To Helen."

> "Helen, they beauty is to me
> Like those Nicean barks of yore,
> That gently, o'er the perfumed sea,
> The weary, way-worn wanderer bore
> To his own native shore."

More often than not, my mother would start by saying, "Hush, Roger," and finally tell him in a loud voice, "SIT DOWN" before he'd had a chance to finish his recitation.

Every Christmas we took a break from unwrapping presents to eat lunch—usually my mother's homemade soup with sherry mixed in for added flavor. Sometimes it was 3:00 or 4:00 in the afternoon before the last present was unwrapped. Then we would pile into several cars and make our way to Sarah Talbot's house for her annual holiday open house. She was one of the town's institutions: a pillar in her church, a patron of the town library, and a sponsor of the local Historical Society. She lived in a big white house at the other end of town.

By the time I was 10, Sarah Talbot was so old that her face had passed from wrinkled to folded, and what hair she had left grew out of her scalp in feathery white wisps. Her ankles had given way, so she walked on the inside edges of her feet and leaned heavily against her walker. She always wore the same off-white, lacy dress with red velvet bows attached to the sleeves. The dress had a train that snaked behind her as she limped along.

We tried to arrive as close to 5:30 as we could before the open house ended at 6:00. This gave us time to give Mrs. Talbot our annual present of a bottle of red wine, wrapped in aluminum foil with a red bow, and to say hello to people before heading back. The youngest child—which in my family was my spot—was expected to shake Mrs. Talbot's hand and kiss her cheek. Her breath always smelled like mold.

As people milled around her house, Mrs. Talbot stayed near her Christmas tree: a perfect specimen from Haggerty's. She didn't believe in conventional Christmas-tree decorations. She covered her tree with small white candles, and hot wax dripped onto the green needles and the floor beneath. I liked to sit near the tree to see if anyone's clothing caught fire. One year, Mrs. Talbot brushed too close to some candles and a piece of her hair sizzled.

Chapter 10
The Patriarch's Summer Estate

My maternal great-grandfather, Frank Artemis Kennedy (and no, not THAT family), was referred to by those of his generation and for three generations to follow as "FAK." He transformed a small family bakery into a booming monopoly with a main factory in Cambridge, Massachusetts and a second factory in Chicago. His company, the Kennedy Biscuit Company, was the first company to make and sell Fig Newton cookies. By the time FAK was in his late 30s, he was a multi-millionaire. He sold his business when in his late 40s to focus on other business enterprises, including buying and selling real estate.

One of his purchases was a property in Vermont, where he created a summer retreat for his family that he called "Buena Vista." The retreat was on a plateau overlooking the Connecticut River on one side and a lake on the other. It had once been a farm and so was comprised of a large lot of land and was located about six miles from Mount Ascutney. I grew up in the original farmhouse, which my mother inherited and where my family lived until I was eighteen years old. FAK had three additional houses built on top of the plateau: two for his children and a grander house—the "Big House"—for himself.

His Big House had sliding pocket doors leading to a long library with floor-to-ceiling bookshelves along one wall. A curved staircase led to the second floor. There was a pink marble sink sitting in a corner of the second floor hallway. One room on that level had a bay window that looked out over the expansive Connecticut River valley below. This was FAK's exercise room, which contained an electric exercise machine that looked like a horse and that rocked back and forth and moved up and down.

FAK liked machines. He owned an electric bridge table that we inherited. By that time its top was torn and its legs shaky, but if you placed a pack of cards in the side slot, plugged the table in, and pushed the button, the table would shake, squeak and quiver, and then shuffle and deal the deck into four hands. He also owned an upright player piano that we stored against the far wall of our barn. Even though the keys were lumpy with barn-swallow guano, the piano still worked. During summer parties my father would insert a paper roll with organized holes in it, and the piano would crank out a tinny tune.

Next to the Big House was a rectangular swimming pool with brick sides. My mother told me that FAK had the pool emptied and filled with fresh water once a week, and that he went swimming in the pool's cool depths every morning at 6 a.m. The pool had no curving walls, no sloping steps, and no shallow section. The walls just went straight down, all around, to a depth of about twelve feet. In one corner, narrow brick-ledge steps protruded outwards into the water so people could climb out. Every spring, his employees would clean the pool and ready it for the summer.

After FAK died no one cleaned and filled the pool anymore or re-mortared the walls when needed. Little plants poked out in some spots, and after it rained, sometimes worms wriggled out from the spaces between the bricks. About twenty years ago, I tried to find the pool. I had to walk through scraggly woods that had reclaimed what had once been a manicured lawn. I found the hole, surrounded by poison ivy. Some of the bricks were still in place. Tree roots protruded on one side, dangling down into the pool like bony vines. Several years later I made the same trip and found that the pool had been filled in with dirt; only a few inches of the top layers of the brick walls were visible.

FAK lived by the clock. He arrived at his estate by July 1st every year and returned to his winter residence in the Boston area right after Labor Day Weekend. While in residence in the country, family members gathered on the croquet lawn in front of his house to get a few games in before the day got too hot. Before lunch, guests and family were herded to the lake for a swim. Then people were free until a late afternoon swimming session at the lake or a tennis game on his grass court. Then they could return to their own homes for dinner.

FAK spent a lot of time improving his vacation property. His workers cleared a path to the lake for easier access, added a series of docks and diving boards, and built two changing rooms—one for men, and one for women—on a flat area before the ground sloped toward the water. A boathouse where his five wooden canoes were stored was on a lower flat spot at the water's edge. FAK ordered roads to be built all over the plateau that were so solidly anchored that years later, you could identify where a road was probably located because of the scar between a row of trees. Once I scratched away the pine needles and a few inches of dirt where I thought a road had been located and found crushed rock and packed clay beneath.

According to family lore, FAK brought electricity to the town, paid for the cost of building a railroad station so he could arrive in his private railroad car, and built many of the small houses around his property so that his gardeners, cooks, chauffeurs, and other employees could live nearby and thus would have no excuse not to get to work on time. When I was in my 20s, I did some research on the town's history and found out that other people and companies deserved the credit for some of these accomplishments. One thing that was true, however, was that he carved a golf course out of the fields that ran along the lake. Sheep from a working farm that he owned south of the town roamed the course to keep the grass munched short. Vermont was sheep country then, and he bred and sold sheep to make a profit. That farm also had a big vegetable garden that supplied fresh produce for his four houses. As children, we were told that important people played golf there, and that the estate was host to many celebrities, including politicians. Bob Labbance confirmed this when he wrote, "Buena Vista was often host to President Woodrow Wilson between 1913 and 1918," (article by Bob Labbance in *Vermont Golf*, 1999).

Despite his self-defined exalted status and his crabby, controlling nature, FAK tried to be thoughtful toward his employees—though he also expected to be obeyed. We have a letter he wrote to his daughter Margrette, my maternal grandmother, in which he encouraged her to be considerate toward his chauffeur. The tone of the letter (written on April 30th, 1915) reveals a lot about his personality:

> "Dear Margrette,
>
> I am sending the car down on Friday, and as the man has to be entirely fitted out, Parker is to be with him so as their uniforms will be alike.
>
> If there have to be any alterations he may not be able to run the car till first of the week.
>
> The man has probably never run a car in Boston, and I also ask you not to run all over the Country, and keep the car on the move continually. You can send the car back when you are finished with the business at hand. The man has a family.
>
> Your affectionate Father."

But he tried to be welcoming to his fellow citizens, sometimes going so far as to allow people from town to play golf on his course at certain times, but he had a lot of rules they had to follow, which he posted here and there along the golf course. Unfortunately, people did not always follow his rules. Once I found a stack of his signs piled up in a corner of our barn that spoke of a disintegrating relationship between FAK and his neighbors.

> "Any person defacing the trees or seats will be barred from coming onto the Golf Grounds."
>
> "NOTICE! Unless the public discontinues the throwing of papers, shells, etc., on the golf grounds, they will be prohibited from entering and walking anywhere within the bounds of the links."

The signs got longer as his patience wore thin.

"It is with great regret that Mr. Kennedy is obliged to call the attention of guests to the misuse of the Golf Course. Large pieces of turf are torn out and not replaced. Every time he goes over the course his pleasure is marred by the carelessness of guests who are supposed to or should know the ordinary rules of golf... It is hoped that beginners will practice on some other Course."

Finally, he withdrew his invitation to let neighbors play on his course.

"Owing to the fact that, after being requested to treat the Golf Grounds in a decent manner, some of the public persist in creating a nuisance in many ways, entering the boathouse, getting in and soiling the boats, littering the greens, cutting the trees and seats, etc., I am obliged to keep out not only this class, but also those who are decent enough to respect private property."

"Owing to the damage to Boat House, Boats and Golf Grounds, all persons are FORBIDDEN TO GO UPON THE LINKS." (The capitalizations are original.)

It always surprises me when I see photographs of FAK, because I had always imagined him to be very tall and commanding but he was short. His wife, on the other hand, was very, very tall: well over 6 feet. She came from Calais, Maine and in the few pictures we have of her, she looks like a female linebacker. The couple had three children: a son and two daughters. Their son Lowell taught mechanical drawing part-time at Harvard. One of their daughters was my maternal grandmother, Margrette, who was six feet tall. Their other daughter, Alice, was six-feet, four-inches tall. She and her husband are the couple in the photograph in our living room that I describe in Chapter 6.

Alice's husband had a drinking problem; once he drank non-stop for over a week and seemed to be failing. The family was in Vermont at the time and knew that the man needed a doctor, but they didn't want to call a doctor who knew them well and who had been practicing medicine for a long time, because then the news might spread about this unhappy situation. After all, the family's honor and reputation were at stake. They called a doctor who had just begun his practice in town and thus was not that well connected to the town's social fabric. The doctor asked about the man's drinking history and was told that he had only been drinking for a few months. "Don't let him drink anymore," he said. The family removed all alcohol from the man's reach and unfortunately, he experienced the DTs and died. Whenever my father told this story, he laughed.

Margrette inherited her father's controlling nature, so the two of them did not get along well. When she was a young woman, she moved in with her aunt who lived several hours away and met and married my grandfather, Sydney: a gentle, mild, and thoughtful man who became a minister. The two of them led a peaceful life, living during the winters wherever his congregations were located and spending the summers in Vermont. They were supposedly teetotalers, but my father told me that they quickly and secretly downed glasses of sherry in the pantry before dinner every night.

FAK's Vermont estate and the bases of his wealth crumbled over time because for two generations after he died, his descendants felt that working for a living was beneath them, and none of them had any financial sense. They made bad investments and lived a lavish lifestyle way beyond their means. When FAK died before the Depression, he was a multi-millionaire. By the time his grandchildren (including my mother) came of age, all that was left was a small annual income combined with an entitled sense of their own place in the world.

When Teddy, Emily, and I grew up, the docks were gone, the changing rooms didn't offer much privacy because their doors had gaping holes, and cash was lacking for needed repairs. Still, the water in the lake was cold and clear. I liked to sit on a side rock at the shore and watch sunfish flicker by. Sunlight slicing down into the shallows turned the waterweeds light green as they flowed back and forth, back and forth with the slow current. Catfish slinked by, picking up bits of sand in their mouths and then spitting the sand out after they had sucked off any algae present. Once a catfish family settled into a nook near the rock. The two adults held guard while the group of seven or eight fry shifted back and forth. They looked a little like tadpoles.

At the edge of the lake, turtles sunned themselves on dead branches that bent from bank to water. Near the water's surface, where the lake lapped up against the beach under a big pine tree, I sometimes found bunches of frogs' eggs encased in jelly sacs. When I walked beyond the sandy beach, my toes sank into the muck. And the woods at the edge of the lake offered cool, damp earth where I could sit down, my back against a tree, and rest.

Storms would pass over the lake and head for land with ferocious energy. Lightning shot down into the water, thunder shook buildings, and rain whipped sideways into windows. Sometimes the rain would turn to hail that would splatter down all over our concrete driveway. It was fun to crunch those ice crystals flat before they melted. Once when I was reading in our living room, a thunderstorm swept in, and a bolt of lightning sparked into a tree at the edge of our yard. The top half of the tree cracked and weaved, and slowly, slowly, began to lean over. Gathering speed, the branches crashed onto the ground. Our gazebo was in the way; part of the roof was flattened, and bits of window frames were thrown clear over to the other side of the lawn.

The entire property consisted of a lot of land, so there was plenty of room for our horses to graze. We were also a doggie family.

My mother loved dogs. She raised Boxers in a big room behind our kitchen. Sometimes we had as many as six to eight puppies, and she laid newspaper all over the floor to catch their pee and poop. That whole end of the house smelled a little like an overflowing toilet. My mother had a special affection for small dogs. Her Pomeranian, Yappy, was the same color as the pillows of our living room couch. One day when he was curled up against one of the couch pillows, an inebriated guest sat on him and smothered him to death. My mother was devastated, though my father thought it was kind of a joke.

My mother chose a darker dog the next time, a Yorkshire terrier that she named "Baby." This dog was hairy and neurotic. He tried to bite my father's calves but had a hard time reaching them. He didn't like going outside when the temperature was colder than 40 degrees Fahrenheit, so a back corner of the living room became his indoor pee spot. My mother would sprinkle some kind of powdered cleaner on the rug, but in damp weather, the entire room reeked of urine. Baby was a picky eater, and my mother used to hand feed him little pieces of steak. We also had a basset hound, Flippity Flop, that would sit mournfully at our feet with her ears dragging and her mouth drooped. She was my dog. I was crazy about her, even though she smelled kind of mangy and slobbered spit.

Our pet dogs went with us everywhere. Flippity preferred the back seat of the car, where she would curl up and dribble and snooze next to me. Baby sat up front on my mother's lap and tried to stick his nose out the window—a tough reach. The dogs even followed us around the house. When I took a bath, Flippity would sit next to the tub and lap water from the toilet bowl. When my mother played bridge, the Boxers lay at her feet. She slept every night with Baby snuggled next to her, with my father relegated to the far side of the bed. Once I lay on the double brass bed in our sleeping porch to read comic books, and I saw fleas leap up from the blanket into the sunlight.

We had a parakeet named Happy who was everyone's pet and who had the run of the house. My mother had a wicker cage that was three feet high and had a top like a pointy hat, but she always kept the cage's door open because she didn't like to see animals caged up. Happy liked to perch on the edges of the books on the living room shelves or on the branches of the tall plant in the dining room. He sat on the edge of the picture window above the kitchen sink when we washed dishes. He would alight onto our shoulders and peck at our hair. One time he walked across my breakfast pancakes, leaving little spiked footprints across the top.

Once a guest held our kitchen door open too long on a cold November day, and Happy flew out into the brittle sunlight. He flittered across our dried-up flowerbeds and settled onto the lower branches of a pine tree at the edge of our yard. We called and called to him, but he wouldn't come inside. He didn't fly to another spot, either, but just stood there on the branch. Finally, Teddy put a ladder next to the tree to get Happy down. He had to break the branch that Happy was standing on, because the bird's little feet were so cold that they had cramped in place. Once he had warmed up in the house, he was able to move around again.

My mother liked Bantam chickens—she thought they were elegantly colored and fashionable, and she told me once that it was good that they ate ticks—so we always owned six or eight hens and a rooster. The hens ran freely all over the yard, laying their eggs under trees or even in the geraniums on our back patio. At the end of the day, the chickens would roost in the horse barn behind our house. The rooster would wake us at dawn with his crowing. I can't remember what happened to the chickens in the winter, but I would not be surprised if they ended up on our dining room table. In the summer months, we kept a pig or two in a low shed on a small hill at the side of the house. In front of the shed was a small, fenced-in area that had been dug out of the earth and where the pigs could roam. One of my jobs as a child was to walk to the shed along the shaded path to feed soggy bread and wilted lettuce to the pigs. Every fall, the butcher would come and take the pigs away, and a few days later, neatly packaged meat would appear in our freezer on the shelf below my mother's frozen casseroles.

Once in the late fall after the pigs had been carted away, Flippity Flop went missing for over 24 hours. I was frantic with worry. During the first day, I stood outside the house every few hours and called her name, but she never appeared. On the second morning, I went out to look for her. As I was walking on the path leading to the pig shed, calling her name, she answered me with a low, moaning bark. I found her in the empty pig yard. I have no idea to this day how she ended up there, but she and I had a joyful reunion.

Next to the pig shed, an old, two-story storage building was altered into a kennel, with pens inside and fenced runways outside. This became home for a pack of foxhounds that my father and one of his friends bought together. To keep the pens clean, we would throw the hounds' messes over the fence into the bushes, hose the running spaces, and throw fresh straw all around.

The foxhounds were purchased with a plan in mind. Several times a summer, fifteen or twenty people drove their horse trailers to our house. By 9 a.m., trucks and empty horse trailers filled our driveway and the horse paddock beyond. People readied themselves between 9:00 and 10:00 a.m., changing into their hunting clothes in our house, and grooming and tacking up their horses. The men wore dressy, dark riding jackets. The older women wore skirts and rode sidesaddle, and their younger counterparts, like my sister, wore haunch-clinging britches and sat astride their mounts. My father

My father, ready for a foxhunt.

wore his red hunting jacket so that people could easily recognize him in the field. After all, he was Master of the Hunt.

My mother would walk among the horses, offering the riders sweet biscuits and coffee laced with Irish Whisky. People exchanged news as they nibbled and drank, and a soft murmur filled our yard, interspersed with the sound of horses' hooves thumping the earth. At 10:30 the hounds were released, and my father blew his fox horn. We didn't have many foxes in Vermont at the time, so the hounds would often chase the scent of deer. It didn't matter, because the noise, speed, and camaraderie were the same. Dust filled the air as the horses raced off, kicking up dirt and sod. The riders would be gone for two or three hours as they raced through the land on top of the plateau, and sometimes we could hear the fox horn's song if they neared our house.

We owned the foxhounds for three or four years until my father's partner, the Joint Master of the Hunt, had a heart attack during one of the hunts and fell dead to the ground. His horse followed the galloping crowd for nearly a quarter of a mile before someone noticed that the rider was missing. My father had a hard time giving up the hounds. For years afterwards, he kept one or two hounds in that pen and took them out riding with him "for memory's sake."

We children had the primary responsibility of helping my father muck out the horse stalls, polish his silver flask that hung from his saddle, and clean the tack. My father's saddle had been specially made to fit the contours of his buttocks and thighs, and it had to be cleaned nearly every time he used it. The braided reins of his bridle were cut generously in order to fit his large hands, and it took extra effort to remove the dirt, horse's hair, and sweat that were caught between the ridges. My father liked to see a high polish on his black, knee-high hunting boots with the brown leather tops. He wanted all of his leather goods to be cleaned and polished as often as possible, including the leather pouch that held his wire cutters, so he could snip fences that got in his way.

I knew how to clean leather before I learned how to wash my own clothes. I knew how to treat a saddle that had been dampened by rain before I could sew on a button. I was cleaning out stalls before I was asked to pick up my own room. I could make a hot-bran mash for the horses on a cold winter evening before I could cook myself an egg. The sweet smell of horses and the rank odor of wet hounds soaked into our shirts, our pants, our hats, and our coats. I'm sure neighbors knew when one of us was coming before the person rounded the corner, just from the person's horsey smell.

One of the stalls in the horse barn was set aside for hay and our tools: the wheelbarrow, manure fork, shovel, and hayfork. We cleaned out the stalls every day by removing wet bedding and horse manure and spreading out some of the dry shavings that were piled on the sides. We would cart the manure to the back of the stable building, where it piled up. The manure pile was a great place to look for worms for fishing, because the lower layers were so moist and pungent. Once every week or two from spring through fall, we emptied each stall down to the dirt floor beneath and then put a week's worth of shavings in the middle and at the sides. In the winter, we let the drier shavings deepen into piles, and every spring we had to empty the stalls of a foot or more of packed bedding.

When the manure pile grew into a cone three or four feet high, my father hired Burt Flood to remove it. Mr. Flood owned a construction business and admired my father, so he was usually available to tackle projects on the property. When a thunderstorm pitted the dirt road leading down the hill to the lake, he would come with his crew to repair the damage. When we had to put a horse down because it had broken a leg or was too arthritic to survive the coming winter without crippling pain, Mr. Flood dug a deep hole in our stable yard with his equipment, and my father led the horse into the open grave. A vet was there to give the animal the fatal injection, and the horse died inside the hole. Then Mr. Flood used his bulldozer to cover up the corpse with displaced earth. Over the years, our stable yard became an unmarked equestrian graveyard.

Another barn was located in front of the house, across the driveway. The only creatures that lived there were barn swallows and big, black, plump hairy spiders that wove intricate, lace-shaped webs in dark corners. On cool mornings, the webs were covered with drops of drew that hung suspended and sparkled like quivering diamonds.

We used the upstairs of the barn for storage. In one corner was a heap of broken bowls and plates, waiting for the glue. White quilts my mother had ordered were stored in plastic bags. In the catalogue, they had looked shiny and decorative, with their little gold stars. But when my mother unwrapped the box, she thought they looked cheap. She saved them, anyway, in case she needed them for guests. We washed them every fall.

We stacked furniture on the first floor—pieces that were broken and awaiting repair, or pieces that were in good shape but not needed at the moment, like the bunk beds my mother figured she might use one day, or the lamp my father didn't like. Our summer furniture pieces—the wicker-seated rockers and iron side tables that FAK had owned—were in the pile in one corner. Every spring we spray-painted the rockers green and white and the tables black, and my father distributed the pieces on the flat land above the pond or on our lawn—some under the shade of trees, others near the flowerbeds—so guests could sit there on warm summer afternoons and watch us play croquet with the family set. The croquet balls were faded and some of the mallets were cracked, but we would never have considered replacing it. After all, the set had once belonged to FAK. "Old but good quality," my father used to say.

The rest of the downstairs of the barn was divided into two areas of unequal size. The larger room had wainscoted walls and a thin-slatted wood floor and had once housed FAK's many automobiles as well as his carriages. When I was growing up, there were only two carriages left: his surrey with the dusty-yellow fringe on top, and the rickshaw he had brought back with him after a trip around the world. We never used the surrey, but we cleaned it every spring, anyway, so guests could sit in it during summer garden parties. We knew that the rickshaw still worked, because sometimes during weekend parties at our house my father or another male guest would pull my mother around the neighborhood in it. They thought the neighbors might enjoy seeing her in her party dress, surrounded by her admiring guests. She even waved a little to people she knew—gently, but with an understated flourish.

The smaller side of the barn contained a long workbench and a concrete-floored station for working on cars. A toilet was installed in a closet in back, so hired help and members of our own family who were outside working didn't have to go into the house, carrying grass and clumps of dirt on their shoes. On the wall next to the bathroom was a tool-sharpening whetstone that my father used by rotating the wheel with his feet. Shelves along the wall held cans of automobile oil and house paint. My father left the brushes there all winter, and in the spring we had to throw most of them out, because the bristles would be permanently bent sideways.

Tools hung above the workbench: each hammer in its own place, and the screwdrivers in a perfect row, from long to short. Nails and screws were stored in labeled coffee cans, and a long broom leaned up in the corner, next to the post hole digger and the lawn rakes. A sickle and scythe hung on the wall in another corner.

My father kept a yellow legal pad on the barn workbench, attached to a clipboard nailed to the wooden surface, where he listed the regular chores. He tied a pencil to the board so at a moment's notice he could add an extra task. On weekends during the school year and during the summer, he expected us to check the pad every morning before we made other plans for the day.

Pine trees grew along the edge of the lawn, and their branches extended over the concrete driveway. We swept the concrete once a week to get rid of the sticky needles. Our lawn was large and sloped at one side down to the street. In the summer, the grass had to be mowed every four or five days. Hedges surrounding the house in the front had to be clipped to keep their shape. And someone had to weed the flowerbeds in back of the house. My father liked us to wash his saddle pads and rope girths in a big tin washtub every month or so and then hang them to dry along the post and rail fence near the stable. Now and then, he would ask us to vacuum bird droppings off the front seat of the rickshaw in the barn.

The list also contained jobs that we didn't have to tackle on a regular basis: repair a pasture fence or take the flagpole down and repaint the eagle on top a shiny gold. Once or twice a year, Teddy climbed to the roof of the barn to spray-paint the rooster-shaped weather vane—the same vane that my husband Jeff painted the first time he met my parents.

We had to work hard to keep up with FAK's example. "He'd turn over in his grave," my father often said, "if he could see the place now." A local farmer hayed the fields, but he accepted a percentage of the bales for pay, which was a break for the family's strained pocketbook. Sometimes when a lot of work had to be done, my father hired a handyman for a day or two, but most of the time he felt that our family should be able to handle the chores. When we finished a task, we checked it off the list. My father supervised us closely and looked at the list at the end of the afternoon, after he had relaxed from his workday and had had a cold beer. Sometimes he would write comments next to certain tasks: "The barn floor looks great, but the shelves are still dusty," or "Give my saddle an extra scrubbing tomorrow; it looked a little grimy last week," or "Please sweep the driveway early on Friday morning, before our weekend guests arrive."

That chore list seemed to suffer from some sort of growth hormone—especially in the summer. It was hard to keep up. Finally, when my brother and sister were in their 20s and no longer living with us, it was clear I couldn't handle all the tasks by myself, so my father hired a yard boy to help me attack the chores. One worked for us two days a week from the time he was 12 until he was about 16. He loved to drive our sit-down mower. Sometimes he would run it very slowly and in straight lines; other times he would drive the machine quickly around in circles. When he was finished, grass stuck up in tufts here and there, while some sections of the lawn were mown down to the dirt.

My father tried to get the yard boy to come more than twice a week but he wasn't interested, so more and more of my time was sucked up with chores. Still, the chore list grew to be two or three pages long. After I went away to college and after my parents had moved to another house in a nearly village (which I explain later), it was time to hire a professional.

Henry Larkin fit the bill. He was in his 50s and made a living by doing odd jobs for people like mowing their lawns, repairing doors, and installing and removing storm windows. My father knew that Henry was trustworthy because when he was younger, he had been Town Constable of the small, nearby village where he lived. Henry agreed to work for my parents one or two days a week in July and August but not on weekends, when he had singing engagements at local restaurants or small parties. He played the guitar fairly well and had a repertoire of country and western songs that he sang in a smooth, lilting tenor. His hair was impressive: so uniformly black that in hindsight I am sure he had dyed it. And he brushed it up into a lump in the front so that it looked a little like a pompadour.

Despite the fact that Henry could not come every day, my father was glad to have his skilled assistance, and Henry was happy to work for us because it gave him steadier income. Henry had a very strong Vermont accent and he spoke quickly, so it took us a week or two to become skilled at understanding the gist of whatever he was saying. Many words that were one syllable became two or three syllables coming out of his mouth. "Spoons" became "SPOOwans," with the accent on the first syllable. Sometimes, though, syllables disappeared—like "BACHler" instead of "bachelor."

My grandmother would have been proud of Henry, because he, too, did not believe in spending a lot of money or wasting resources. He thought people used too much water by bathing more than once a week. "Fridays 'er my BATHin' day," he told me once, "and if I go SWIMen' on WENsday or THURsday, I SKIPawee." Henry's village was about six miles from my parents' house. Once my father had to pick Henry up for work because his car had broken down; I was home from college so went with him for the ride. Henry invited us in. His living room was full of extra chairs that he had stacked neatly against the walls. A large cardboard box held all the flatware he had been lucky to collect in garage sales over the years. "You NEvah know when you my nee'a few EXtrah SPOOwans," he explained. "This house nees a WOMan's tetch," he added. "This HEahs whatcha call a BACH'ler pad."

Henry approved of the piles of chairs, beds, bureaus, tables, and old skis, stored in the barn. He owned three refrigerators: one was in his house, one on his sagging back porch, and one on his lawn. If the one in the house stopped working, he had replacements on hand. He drove a rusty, light gray car that had had only 56,000 miles on it when he bought it. But what if the radiator cracked? Or brakes had to be replaced? Henry was not sure he would have the financial resources to pay for the work that would be needed, so to be safe, he stockpiled bits and pieces of old cars that he had bought from a local junkyard and stored them at the edge of his lawn. He also collected old tires and extra car batteries.

Henry started his work for my parents with a bang. He whittled down our chore list to a reasonable length and even instituted some useful innovations, like removing the paintbrushes from the turpentine and storing them flat so they would not have to be replaced every year. But by the beginning of August, my father was beginning to suspect that Henry wasn't working hard enough. The floor in the barn connected to the house was sometimes still dusty in the corners, and the barn windows were not as clean as he liked. The chore list wasn't getting any shorter; in fact, it had begun to grow again. My father had thought that a grown man would accomplish more, and he was disappointed.

He decided it was time to go over the items on the chore list more carefully with Henry on the mornings he came to work. Perhaps this would help Henry understand the importance of all the tasks and set his priorities in a more efficient manner. My father even began to estimate how long each job should take to complete, and he wrote these times next to each item on the list. In the first few days of this new arrangement, Henry listened carefully and quietly, but after a few days my father's directions grew more elaborate and Henry grew restless. There was so much to do, and he wanted to get to work instead of listening for 30 to 45 minutes before he could attack the chore list. And my father was not being realistic about how long it took to get things done.

Henry started to question the need for some of the jobs. If he could shorten the list, then he could concentrate on more of the important items. In the interests of being fair, my father at first agreed with some of Henry's points, but he still insisted that most of the chores remain on the list. One morning, Henry said, "Then FLOWabeds don't need trimmin', 'cause I DUN tha last wee." My father had to put his foot down and insist. Guests were arriving that afternoon, and the front of the house had to look presentable. Henry pouted for the rest of the morning and left work early that afternoon.

The next day, as they reviewed the list together, Henry said, "Washin them barn WINdows doe need DOOwan. I also dun THA' las'WEE."

This defiance was the last straw. My father fired him on the spot. Henry told everyone he had quit because my father was too bossy.

Chapter 11
Our Town

Once when I was a child and alone at home, I thought the Dutch door leading from our kitchen to the patio was unlocked. I pushed against the top pane of glass to open the door, and my hand went through the glass. I had two deep cuts in my palm and still carry slight scars from that injury today, some 65 years later. I ran across the street to the Flints' house, where Mrs. Flint took care of me. I remember eating her cookies while she removed some glass from my hand, disinfected the wound, and wrapped my hand in bandages.

Mr. Flint owned the furniture store on South Main Street. He specialized in bunk beds and floor lamps, and his collection of lampshades looked like fancy hats with bows in the middle and lace at the edges. The Flints had a son—Eddie—who was a few years younger than I was. Eddie worshipped my brother Teddy. Nearly every morning in the summer, Eddie would drop by our house to see if Teddy had any chores for him to do, like helping him clean his room or sweep the driveway. Sometimes Eddie would just follow Teddy around, but it was great to have his help when needed. After Teddy moved into his own place, Eddie stopped visiting us.

My mother's favorite supermarket was Fortunes' Market, located about a half mile from our house and tucked into the bank of a large stream that led from the lake near our house into the Connecticut River. The Fortunes lived four or five houses down the street from our house. Bill Fortune was a chunky, friendly man who wore short-sleeved work shirts and brown shoes. When he chuckled, his stomach shook. His wife Edna had light brown hair that curled softly against her round face. Their only child, Floyd, had big ears that stuck out from the sides of his head, and he wore his long, greasy hair brushed back from his face and tied in the back. He spent most of the day unloading cartons of food, stacking cans on the shelves, and filling the cooler with milk and orange juice. Now and then, he would help a customer carry groceries to the car.

My mother went to Fortunes' Market nearly every day to pick up something she needed. Why go to the supermarket at the other end of town and stand in line for a loaf of bread or a bottle of juice? Mr. and Mrs. Fortune also sold small bottles of wine that were stacked neatly in the back of the store, and cold beer was always available in the cooler. If we ran out of quinine water or needed a lemon or lime for gin and tonics, my mother could ask my brother, sister, or a family guest to drive down the hill to pick up the purchases. She would call ahead and have Edna or Bill ring up the items and bag them in advance.

Fortunes' Market also gave us credit, while at the supermarket we were expected to pay on the spot. We probably spent more money at Fortunes' Market than we did at any other store, and it was a poor investment. The supermarket carried soda water in plastic gallon jugs, but my mother liked the glass quarts at Fortunes, even though they cost more. And the store had a markup for beer and wine that was probably north of 10%.

I loved Fortunes' Market: the candy in glass jars on the counter, the cooler full of ice cream and popsicles, a shelf devoted solely to Twinkies and chocolate muffins with creamy centers, and a comic book display. I used to walk there almost every day during the summer to buy a fudgsicle. I took my time going home, lingering on the bridge near the store and enjoying my treat. I liked to watch the white water fall over an old dam that was right before the bridge. Sometimes I sat on the curb to look at an ant carry a big crumb or drag the leg of a dead bug across the sidewalk.

When I was about nine or ten years old, I was having a particularly bad summer at home. My parents were still hosting many parties but also fighting with each other a lot. With all the traffic in and out of our house, Mrs. Deller was not able to keep up with the housework, so the house was disorganized and messy. I was alone a lot, and most nights I ate TV dinners by myself; my mother would put a pre-packaged dinner on a small, metal collapsible table. I can still envision some of those meals: bits of brown meat floating in thick gravy in one slot, peas in another slot, and a mound of mashed potatoes with a blob of butter on top in the last slot; or a slab of dried-up fish wrapped in bread crumbs in one slot, rice in the slot next door, and canned green beans in the last section. The beans were always soft and tasted waxy. My brother and sister were a decade older than I was, and when they were home, they spent most of the time with their friends and didn't pay much attention to me. Life was unfair. I decided it was time to run away from home.

I thought carefully about what I would need. I scooped up some pennies from my father's coin dish on his bureau and put them in the bottom of a small paper bag. I found a clean pair of socks and some extra Kleenex. I made myself a peanut butter and jelly sandwich in case I got hungry. I tried to find a bandanna to tie around my head so I would look like a hobo, but I had to settle for one of my father's linen handkerchiefs. It was too small to wear, so I put it in the paper bag on top of the sandwich. I figured I could use it to wipe sweat off my face. I was ready to go.

I walked slowly down the hill toward town. *They'll be sorry when they find out I'm gone,* I thought. My mother would call me for dinner, and I wouldn't answer. My father would want to compliment me on how well I had swept the driveway, but I couldn't be found. Emily would feel guilty that she hadn't played that game of cards with me before I left. And Teddy would regret that he hadn't taken me swimming at the lake. They would become frantic and call around the neighborhood, but no one would know where I was.

It was a hot afternoon. As I trudged along, the sun baked the still air. The trees seemed immobile in the heat, and my bag got heavier and heavier. Just thinking about how unfair my family was and how little they appreciated me helped me keep my spirits up. Still, by the time I reached the bottom of the hill, I was weeping with self-pity. It had taken a lot out of me to leave home. I looked up and saw the Fortunes' Market sign. I groped in the bag and took out all the money. I didn't have enough to buy a fudgsicle, but I could always charge it to our account.

The store was a busy place so people didn't seem to notice the state I was in. I went back outside with my fudgsicle and lingered by the bridge. By the time I was finished, I was feeling better. I decided that I had been gone long enough to teach my family a lesson. It was time to go home. It was a long way back up that steep hill, though, and the day was even hotter than it was when I had started my journey. I went back into the market and asked Floyd to call my house, so I could get someone to drive down and pick me up. I knew my family would be relieved to hear from me, and I was ready to be forgiving.

"Oh, it's great that you're there," my father said, when Floyd handed me the phone. "Your mother will be down in twenty minutes. Can you pick up some soda water and a few lemons? We just ran out."

When I got a little older, I traveled beyond Fortunes' Market to the stores in the middle of town. Walking into Mr. Cushing's drugstore, I passed the cosmetics and newspapers on one side and the pharmacy counter on the other. The soda fountain ran along the back of the rear wall. Mr. Cushing had a machine that made delicious ice cream frappes. He put heavy cream, ice cream, and flavored syrup into a tall metal cup and then put the cup under a big mixing device. There was always enough in the metal cup for a glass and a half of chilly frappe, so thick and rich that the bubbles used to sit unbroken on the surface.

Ice cream sundaes were my favorite. In the fall of my sixth grade year, I walked past Cushing's Pharmacy as often as I could on my way home after school. By 3:30, I was sitting on the stool, giving my order: two scoops of vanilla ice cream in a stemmed glass dish, with thick, hot fudge glopped on top, the whipped cream, and finished off with a cherry. I tried to eat it before the fudge turned cold. Sometimes, one sundae wasn't enough, and I ate two. My meager allowance did not cover this treat five days a week, but sometimes I was able to squeeze a few quarters or a dollar or two from one of my parents.

Every day Mr. Cushing would ask, "What'll it be, young lady?" He wanted to give me a chance to pick a marshmallow instead of a cherry, or to substitute strawberry ice cream. But I was stuck in my ways. Finally, at the end of May, one month before school was over for the year, I had lost my hunger for hot-fudge sundaes. By then, I had gained 12 pounds.

When I was in elementary school, Hannah Brown was my best friend. I spent a lot of time in her tall, skinny green house that backed up against the schoolyard fence. During the school week, we would sometimes sneak through a hole in the fence to have lunch in her kitchen. Her mother would be waiting with warm soup—usually tomato—and some kind of sandwich for each of us. Her grilled cheese sandwiches were my favorite; I can still see one on a plate, with the cheese oozing out beyond the bread's crusts.

On weekends, Hannah and I would retreat to my bedroom to read romance comic books that I stored in a box under my bed. I didn't mind inviting Hannah to my house because I knew that her mother had an issue with alcohol, too, so I was sure that Hannah wouldn't be shocked about what went on in my house. I was right; she just took it all in stride.

Hannah and I liked to go the movies. Before the theater in town burned down, its roof sagged to the right, its front door was cracked, and the ticket window was caked with dirt. The chairs inside were ripped and covered with cigarette holes. Still, we tried to go to the Saturday matinee as often as we could, when my mother could drive us there and pick us up afterwards. We would stop at Fortunes' Market on the way to charge some junior mints and pompoms to my family's account. I would gobble down the candy while I watched Mickey Mouse cartoons or movies like "Chitty Chitty Bang Bang." One of our favorite movie stars was Connie Francis. Once, when we were watching *Where the Boys Are*, in which she was the star, there was a downpour outside the theater, just as young people on the screen ran onto the beach under the Florida sun. We had to move our seats because water was pouring through the roof, down the aisle near our row, and splashing up against our shoes. It was hard to hear Connie sing above the cascade.

Sometimes the theater offered a double feature. Once we asked my mother if she would drive us to the theater so we could see *The Teenage Werewolf*, playing with a partner movie about invaders from outer space. My mother said "Sure." After all, with the word "teenager" in the title, how harmful could the movie be?

I clutched the armrests of my seat as Michael Langdon grew whiskers and pointy ears and leapt out growling from behind trees to scare women and children passing by. As for the second feature, I shuddered when two-foot high aliens with heads like balloons and legs like sticks danced in a circle in the moonlight and made high-pitched squealing noises. They could extend their fingernails at will, and alcohol dripped from their nails. An alien's hand could disconnect from the wrist and wriggle to the prey. In one scene, a teenage boy and girl were necking in the front seat of his car when a disembodied hand slithered up the back of the seat, nails extended, and injected the boy in the neck.

Hannah laughed heartily through both movies. She thought Michael Langdon was cute, even with hair all over his nose. And she especially liked the scene in the second movie when the aliens injected a herd of cows. All the animals fell over at the same time, with their legs sticking straight up into the air. But for weeks after I saw these movies, I avoided walking by the stairs leading to our third floor because I thought I could see the werewolf's shadow on the wall of the landing above. I found it hard to open my closet at night in case a hand with nails dripping alcohol was waiting under one of my shoes.

If Hannah and I were lucky, her older brother would take us to the drive-in movie, seven miles out of town. Movies there started at 8:30 p.m. in the summer, after it was dark enough to see the screen. At the drive-in, we didn't have to worry about making noise that would bother other moviegoers. We could chat during the movie and get out of the car if we wanted to order French fries at the concession stand. The fries were greasy, and after eating some, I felt as if I had spread butter on my lips. I can still see that ad right before the intermission, during which a hot dog with legs danced across the screen, pointing to the concession stand with arms that looked like little brown twigs.

Sometimes before the drive-in movie started, we would eat dinner at Hannah's house. Her family ate together at 6:30, while at my house I ate around 7:00 and my parents around 8:00. Hannah's father owned an electric knife that slid its way through roast beef. He approached the meat the way a surgeon might approach a patient on the operating table: studying its surfaces, turning the platter this way and that until he found the perfect entry point. He stood a respectful distance from the table, and with the confidence of a trained professional, turned the knife on and created slice after perfect slice that curled over into a neat stack on the plate. The knife whirred quietly. He always wore a sparkling white apron when he carved, and when he was done, the apron would still be clean.

My father was quite the contrast. He would sharpen our old, bone-handled carving knife on the round knife sharpener, stab a roast with the chipped, matching fork, and hack away. The pieces of roast that my father carved would be thick at one end and thin at the other, with ridges in between of red, quivering meat. Hannah's family members ate their meat medium to well done. Not in my family. We were hearty hunters who knew the restorative power of blood. My mother liked red meat so rare that, as she used to say, the center would be "just kissed with heat." When my father was through carving the roast, bloody juice would be splattered on his hands, wrists, and shirtfront, and the carving board would be covered with red-stained digs and scrapes.

Hannah and I were in the same homeroom together in school and spent a lot of time together from September to June. Danny Perkins was my special summer friend. His family lived in New York City but spent every July and August in a big gray house at the other end of town. Danny was the youngest in his family, like me. I couldn't imagine a summer without him.

Danny's mother and father played bridge with my parents, so they knew about the goings-on at my house. Danny's mother was short and wiry, had salt and pepper hair cut close to her head, and walked with quick, bird-like twitches, her head held stiffly to the side. She dressed in baggy khaki pants, usually dirty from her garden work, and her feet seemed always encased in dusty sneakers with holes in the toe. My mother did not approve of the look. She thought that

Danny's father was more elegant: he always wore a dress shirt and a bow tie, even on the hottest days.

Danny had two older brothers. Joshua hoped one day to go into the priesthood because he liked listening to Gregorian Chants. He quoted Byron's poetry and talked a lot about God. Danny's other brother, Alexander, had bushy hair on his arms and chest. He tied his long, dark hair back with a ribbon and left his shirts half-open in front. Sometimes his chest hair got tangled up in the shirt's top buttons. When he walked, he would place one foot carefully in front of him, and his muscled leg would follow. When he pointed, his arm would flex. High school girls in town would stare at him in unabashed worship.

Danny and I were friends throughout our childhoods. He spent a lot of time at our place, playing tennis on the old clay court my great-grandfather had built or swimming in the lake. Danny was a good swimmer, flashing like a fish through the water. He was also a good runner—graceful and athletic. When Danny and I washed my parents' car, his wrists and elbows swayed with liquid elasticity as he sponged off the hood.

My friend Hannah thought Danny was just a dreamboat. By May first, she was talking about him all the time and counting the days until his family arrived from New York City. She liked to sit in her room and listen to "Johnny Angel," whispering the lyrics softly, and substituting "Danny" for "Johnny."

I used to imagine that Hannah dreamed up all sorts of plans so she and Danny could be alone together. I could invite them both to dinner at my house, and while we were sitting down to hamburgers and pickles, with mustard on the bun—one of Danny's favorites—I would be called away. My grandmother had died, or my father had broken his leg. They would be kind about it, and understand. Or the three of us might go for a picnic at the lake, and then I would offer to pick up the plates and cups, to leave the two of them alone. Perhaps Hannah might cut her foot on a sharp rock, and Danny would have to carry her from the lake to the emergency room. He could hold her hand while she was waiting to be treated. Hannah had a romantic nature, but even that idea of mine was unrealistic, since the hospital was four miles from the lake, and at that time, Danny wasn't that much taller than Hannah.

Chapter 12

A Fresh Start?

In the fall of my 7th grade year, my parents moved to another town where the Equestrian Club was located: about 15 miles away from our house, and I had to leave Hannah behind. My father was managing the Club at the time. The road between the Club and our house was full of high hills and sharp corners, as well as a few bars, so his 35-minute commute had obstacles and enticements that often made him late returning home for dinner. The problem worsened when a thin layer of ice covered the roads. Sometimes when it was snowing hard, my father would spend a night or two at an inn near the Club. My mother worried about what he might be up to and thought it would make things easier for everyone if my father worked closer to where we lived. I realized years later that she also might have worried about his relationship with his mistress—a relationship that may have started around that time.

One September afternoon when my father was having a beer with his friend and fellow Club member, Mr. Rutland, he was lamenting the pressure my mother was putting on him to move our family closer to the Club or to find another job that wasn't so far from our house. Mr. and Mrs. Rutland were deeply committed to the Club. They owned four horses and participated in all the Club's competitions. Mr. Rutland liked to display his horse and buggy, and he always hung small American flags on the top of the carriage seat. Mr. Rutland thought that all Democrats were Communists, and whenever a Democrat won any election, he hung his American Flag at half-mast on the flagpole in his yard.

Mr. Rutland rode western, like a cowboy. This was an embarrassment to the other members of the Club, who rode hunt seat: sitting astride with legs bent and reins held separately in both hands, wrists flexed, fingers curled inward, shoulders down, back straight, and head held so they looked directly ahead. The first time I saw a ballet dancer perform, I thought that from the waist up, her posture was the same as if she were sitting astride a horse. In comparison, Mr. Rutland sat leaning back on his stock saddle. The usual outfit at the Club was formal wear: Jodhpur pants, white shirts, and in cool weather, a dark fitted jacket. Mr. Rutland wore a leather jacket with fringe hanging off the sleeves. He held the reins in one hand so he could wave to Club members as he trotted by. The fringe on his sleeves swayed back and forth as he moved his arm.

Most wives in the Equestrian Club were friendly and polite but a little remote and formal. Mrs. Rutland was loud in comparison. She slapped a man on the back once, to congratulate him for winning first place in a jumping class. She even went so far as to challenge my father now and then about a decision he had made as judge. She didn't speak to him quietly and carefully after the ribbons were awarded. Instead, she would walk right up to the judge's table and speak to him in her booming voice. But my father forgave her and the Club members put up with Mr. Rutland's riding style, because the Rutlands were rich and generous, which was important to the Club's financial health. Mr. and Mrs. Rutland contributed money every year and gave a gift large enough to help fund the construction of a new building of horse stalls.

The Rutlands loved New England summers but found the winters difficult. They lived five miles from the Equestrian Club at the edge of an isolated dirt road. Other than their caretaker, who lived in a small house on their property and looked after the grounds and horses, their closest neighbor was several miles away. Sometimes after a big snowstorm, the town plows didn't get to their house for a day or two. The electricity and phone system had gone out in a blizzard two years before, and it was three days before power was restored. If Mr. Rutland hadn't installed his own generator for such an emergency, they would have run out of water, because their well had an electric pump. Spring seasons were hard, too, when the dirt road in front of their brick Colonial filled with mucky ruts, and even their four-wheel-drive Jeep sometimes got stuck.

They began to spend a few months in Florida in the winter in a home they had purchased that was near the ocean. One year they considered living there from October to May, to see if they missed New England. Mr. and Mrs. Rutland were not ready yet, though, to commit to spending that much time in Florida in the winter until they found someone who would watch over their Vermont house while they were away. The caretaker would remain behind, but he still needed close supervision because he had a drinking problem (how ironic). Over their third beers one afternoon, Mr. Rutland and my father came up with an answer to both their dilemmas. The two men decided that we would live in the Rutland house over the winter, and in return, we would only have to pay for the utilities. The house had a large living room and five bedrooms, so we could still have overnight guests. And we could bring our own horses, because there were seven empty stalls in the Rutlands' barn.

I didn't want to move. Hannah and I had just started seventh grade in the new middle school, located at the back of the high school. It felt special to walk past the older students on our way to homeroom, and we could use the high school's library and its shiny, new gym. I knew that seventh graders in Mr. Rutland's town had classes in an older building, next to babies in grades one through six. But I didn't have a vote, so we packed our bags, loaded the horses into vans, closed up our house, and settled into the Rutlands' house in mid-October.

I knew I was in trouble on my first day in my new school. I got lost finding my homeroom, so I was five minutes late. My new homeroom teacher, Mr. Hopkins, made me stand against the hallway wall outside the room. "Don't move," he told me, shaking his index finger in my direction. "Not a twitch." His finger wobbled as he pointed. He left me there for ten minutes before he let me into the room.

Mr. Hopkins was tall and had white hair that was cut close to his scalp. When he sat at his desk, we could see his scalp wrinkle underneath the fuzz when he moved his eyebrows, which he did whenever he felt strongly about whatever he was saying.

In addition to running our homeroom, Mr. Hopkins taught social studies. He had turned to education after a long stint in the army, and he applied the lessons he had learned in the military to his teaching. Students had to be at their desks, hands folded, papers put away, by 8:15 a.m. sharp. No one was allowed to talk. No notes were passed, and no one wriggled. Mr. Hopkins liked to start the day with five minutes of silence, and then we stood and recited the Pledge of Allegiance. If we did not speak with one voice, we repeated it again. One morning it took us four tries before he was satisfied.

If we had time after he read the announcements, he would elicit one or two questions from one or two students in our homeroom. He thought the job of asking questions was a skill people should learn, and therefore a skill that he, as a teacher, had the responsibility to teach. There were twenty-two students in his homeroom, and he would always be sure that each of us had a chance to ask one question at least once a month. He never gave us warning about who would be "up," because he wanted us to learn to think quickly on our feet. Even if we had been asked a question the day before, we were never safe. And not just any question would do. Our questions had to confirm that we had been listening to his announcements or had learned the material we were studying at the time in his social studies class. If Mr. Hopkins thought a question didn't reflect adequate thought and preparation, the student's name was put back on the list for an extra turn that month.

Mr. Hopkins was more interested in the impact strong personalities had on history than on the sequential march of events, so in his social studies class he would jump back and forth from one century to another, and one country to another—a little like a bat darting back and forth at dusk, looking for wandering dragonflies. Until I was in high school, I thought that Caesar and Napoleon might have met each other on the battlefield.

One day in homeroom when student Willy Whittier was back in school after a few days of being at home with the flu, Mr. Hopkins called on him to ask a question. Willy didn't need time to gather his thoughts; he already had a question in mind. "Mr. Hopkins," he asked. "Would our language have been different if the Battle of Hastings hadn't happened?"

We were all impressed. Willy had taken a step beyond the information we had learned to wonder "if." I thought he was brilliant. Unfortunately, Willy didn't know that we had moved on from early English history to Ben Franklin the day before. He was required to ask two more questions that month.

Mr. Hopkins took it as a personal insult if the grades that students in his social studies class earned were not among the highest in the school. And as his homeroom charges, he expected us to set an example by being quiet and respectful at all-school assemblies and to stand up straight in the hallways as we moved from room to room. When we went out to recess, we were to march quietly until the last one of us had left the building. He would come out five minutes before recess was over so we could line up properly for the return journey. Once two boys were late getting into their places in line, and we had to stand for ten minutes against the wall in the sun, with our arms held straight down against our bodies, before Mr. Hopkins let us back inside.

My mother wasn't very happy in the Rutlands' house. My father left early every morning for the Equestrian Club, even before my mother drove me to the school bus stop two miles from the house. And he would often return home late, after dark—sometimes even after the cocktail hour. Other than the caretaker, we had no immediate neighbors, and those that lived a few miles away didn't seem to deserve her attention. When the snow was deep on the road in front of the house, my mother couldn't drive to her weekly bridge games, and my parents were not able to throw as many parties.

My mother decided in early April that it was time to go home. The Rutlands didn't mind that we were leaving early, because they'd had such a great winter in Florida that they'd decided to sell their New England house, buy a larger place in Florida, and move permanently south. They wanted to put the property on the market as soon as possible, and their real estate agent suggested that the property might be more appealing if the house was unoccupied but still furnished—always clean, always neat. No chance of arriving on a Saturday or Sunday with a prospective buyer and finding my parents enjoying a liquid lunch.

But what was to be done about me? I had already switched schools once that year, and it seemed a shame to move me a second time, especially since there were about two and a half months left before summer vacation. And the two schools were very different. In my old school, 7th graders were studying division and reading short stories. In my new school, I had faced pre-algebra, and that spring in our English class, we were reading Hemingway's *The Old Man and the Sea*.

My mother found a place for me to live near the new school so I wouldn't have to leave before the school year was over. I could still go home on weekends, though, and in mid-June, I could return home for good. Before I knew it, my bags were packed and I was moving into the home of the local undertaker, Mr. Morrison.

Mr. and Mrs. Morrison's house was three stories high. The top floor contained two rooms under the eaves: one for storage and the other for guests. The guestroom became my room. The walls sloped up toward a narrow ceiling, and the room only had one dormer window so on hot days, the air in the room was sticky. Mr. and Mrs. Morrison and their two teenage sons lived on the second floor. The kitchen was in back on that level and had orange and yellow wallpaper with pictures of black pots and pans, surrounded by blue flowers.

The family business was located on the first floor. The reception area was in front, where plush, red velvet couches lined the walls. Off the reception room were two large rooms, each with space in the front for the coffins and chairs in the back for family and friends. Each of these rooms had dark wallpaper and subtle lighting. A large driveway and parking lot accommodated the hearses and mourners' cars. The lawn was carefully landscaped to be welcoming to grieving families and friends.

Mr. and Mrs. Morrison put in long days, especially as May turned to June and old people began to die in the swelling heat. The couple would go downstairs right after breakfast, and Mrs.

Morrison came back up around 4:00 to prepare dinner. From my room I could hear her moving pots and pans in the kitchen below. We ate at 5:45 sharp so Mr. Morrison could be present at wakes that usually started at 7:00 p.m.

Before Mr. Morrison sat down at the table, he scrubbed his hands with a special antiseptic soap kept in a plastic box at the side of the kitchen sink. When I go into a hospital, I'm reminded of the soap's smell. Mr. Morrison was a meat and potato man, so we ate meatloaf with boiled potatoes, or steak with French fries, or chicken with mashed potatoes and peas. He liked to talk about his day as we ate, describing how he'd prepared the "departed" for viewings. I used to dream that dead people lurked downstairs, waiting for us to go to sleep so they could rise up and finish off the leftover meatloaf.

I was sick for ten days later that spring. After lying in bed in my attic room for about three days, hearing hearses coming and going and the stairs creaking as Mr. and Mrs. Morrison went up and down, and after eating sandwiches Mrs. Morrison brought me while I sat in bed, I called my parents and begged them to take me home until I was well enough to go back to school.

Before I got sick and afterwards, I always looked forward to going home on weekends, but transportation was sometimes difficult. My father was not always in the area on Friday afternoons, and my mother was often busy preparing for weekend parties. If I couldn't go home, I had to go somewhere, because Mrs. Morrison's sister sometimes visited on weekends and slept in the guest room.

My parents arranged for me to stay some weekends with the Bates family who lived at the other end of town. Mr. Bates and my father were friends because both were involved in the Equestrian Club. The Bates family lived in a big house with a barn attached. Mr. Bates owned eight horses and augmented his income by stabling other people's horses. In the summer, the Equestrian Club rented his fields and barn for Pony Club events. Mr. Bates was a widower and had five children, including his daughter, Sarah. She and I were in the same class at school, so on the Friday afternoons when my parents couldn't pick me up, I went home with her on the school bus. In return, my parents paid Mr. Bates for every weekend I spent in his house. I joined the children in mucking out stalls, cleaning tack, and grooming horses. I didn't mind because it was the same work I did at home, but at least at the Bates' house there were children my own age.

I would have been 100% content except for three problems. First, the screen in the Bates' bathroom window had holes in it and they left a night light on in the room. At night, big hairy moths would fly in and buzz against the walls and the night light. Second, I slept in Sarah's room on a small cot that sagged in the middle. I'm broad shouldered, so I had to scrunch myself up to fit in the canvas sling.

And last, the food we ate. It was awful. Mr. Bates gave weekend parties, too, and served leg of lamb or roast beef with Yorkshire pudding to his guests. We children ate first in the kitchen, and we had different fare—sometimes cereal and toast, or corn on the cob that grew behind the house. Now and then we ate Spam, which came out of a can that we opened by releasing a little metal key that was on top of the can and hooking the key into a strip of metal around the top of the can's sides. Then we turned the key to curl the strip off so we could lift the lid. We would cut the hunk of Spam into slices that we fried and then ate with ketchup or mustard.

I can still see that Spam resting on the plate when it first came out of the can: speckled and pink, with its sides coated with a thin layer of Jell-O-like fat. It looked a little like quivering dog food.

Chapter 13

Financial Struggles

When I was in 8th grade and back in my old school, during winter school vacation and on weekends I spent a lot of time skiing at nearby Mount Ascutney, located six miles from my house. My mother would drop me off in the morning and then pick me up after the ski lifts closed for the day. I used to eat lunch in the ski-hut cafeteria. I especially liked their cheeseburgers served on toasted buns. Sometimes Hannah met me there, and we would have a great time, skiing and gossiping about school.

At first, we knew just about everyone on the slopes, because almost every kid in our school who could ski was there. But after a while things began to change. Out-of-staters had discovered the sport of skiing. We began to see more cars with Connecticut, New Jersey, and New York license plates in the parking lot. People wearing light purple or pink pants, and bushy fake-fur hats put on their bright yellow or blue skis with safety bindings and struggled past us locals with our blue jeans and long-thong bindings. I remember seeing one woman whose shiny orange pants were so tight that I wondered how she could bend her body in order to turn when she skied.

Despite the onslaught of strangers, local people remained loyal to Mount Ascutney, partly because they could get a discount on a season pass: a plastic-covered piece of cardboard with the person's picture stamped on the front. Many local people also worked at the ski area. Walter O'Day, who lived near the ski area on his family farm, got a part-time job there to augment his income. He would sit in the heated hut at the mid-way station where people could choose to get off the lift or continue up to the top. If someone fell onto the ground while getting off the lift, Walter would stop the lift to give the person time to stand up and ski out of the way.

He and his wife Anne owned eight milking cows, raised pigs, and nurtured a vegetable garden that filled the field next to their house. The rows between Anne's beans, peas, corn, and squash were so straight and free of weeds that they looked as if they were made of flat brown cardboard. Anne prided herself on running a tight ship. Her linoleum kitchen floor sparkled, and there was not a visible piece of dust on any table, couch, or chair. Until I saw the inside of their house, I always thought that farmers' houses would be filled with animal droppings, urine-soaked rugs, and buzzing flies inside window panes, the way our house was.

As time passed, the ski area began to lose skiers. Climate change reduced the amount of natural snow the mountain received and limited the number of cold winter nights when snow could be made. The ski lodge became grimy, the food service ended, and the trails were not well groomed. Traffic on the slopes dwindled to a trickle. A couple from a rich suburb of New York City who had enjoyed skiing there when the area was in its prime bought it for a song. They hired all new employees, even replacing Walter O'Day in the mid-way station. And they decided that it wasn't fair to give local people discounts when skiers from New York and Connecticut had to pay full price.

Business seemed to improve a little as out-of-staters kept flooding into Vermont and buying second homes, but people from the local area found the tickets too expensive, the lift lines too crowded, and the new, plastic décor in the lodge unsettling, so a lot of them stopped skiing there. Locals as well as out-of-staters began to prefer the ski area ten miles down the road, which had better snowmaking equipment, cheaper tickets, and a fancier ski lodge. There were also more hotels and motels near the slopes there, where out-of-staters could stay. The slopes at Mount Ascutney emptied out, and the owners finally declared bankruptcy and moved away.

At around the same time, the economy of our town weakened when the two factories in town closed because the companies moved their operations out of state or out of the country. But parties continued at our house: liquor flowing, and my father and guests dragging my mother around the neighborhood in the rickshaw.

Chapter 14

Away at Last

For my 9th grade year, I was sent to a coeducational, independent school and left Hannah Brown behind for good. Woodstock Country School, or WCS, as we called it, was a boarding school that had been carved out of an old dairy farm. The kitchen, dining hall, and community living room used to be the cow barn. Five classrooms were added at one side of the building, the tractor shed was transformed into science labs, and the farmhouse and another old barn became dorms.

WCS was a progressive school, so we called our teachers by their first names. That took some getting used to, I must admit, after being taught to stand up when my parents' friends entered the room, look them squarely in the eye as I firmly shook their hands, and always address them formally by their last names (except for all the "aunts" and "uncles").

In our courses, we learned by doing rather than by memorizing. In our biology class, we took walks across the soccer field to find anything growing wild that could be edible, and one day, we picked unfurled fiddlehead ferns and cooked them in a fire pit we built in the yard outside the dining hall. We also searched the stream near the Main Building for visible evidence of pollution, like toilet paper rolls or empty beer bottles. It wasn't hard to find such evidence. I remember once standing in the stream and seeing a used Kotex menstruation pad float by in the water's currents. And I knew from the time I'd spent at the Equestrian Club that horses urinated and defecated into the stream. Still, in the name of science, we took water samples from that stream every week, looked at them under a microscope, and recorded our observations in our lab notebooks.

Most people I knew from my town, like Hannah, went to the high school on the corner of State and Ascutney Streets in a building that was tall, made of brick, and had windows covered with wire mesh. I thought it looked a little like the state prison on State Street, near the center of town. Hannah had been telling me stories about how boring her classes were. She had to memorize dates in history class, diagram a sentence into its grammatical parts in language arts, and know the names of the bones in the human body in biology. I was glad I wasn't going to that school.

WCS was located 45 minutes from my house. When I was in 9th grade, I was a commuting or "day" student. There were only five day students in the school, and three of us lived within 15 minutes of each other. The three families formed a car pool to share the commuting burden. The school had a special room above the administrative offices where day students could sit in the late afternoon and wait for their rides home. When it was my parents' turn to pick up the three of us, my father or mother would invariably be late, so we sometimes sat up in that room for an hour or more. And more than once, my father arrived with alcohol on his breath. After a few months, I was kicked out of the car pool. Then my parents had to drive me up and back every day until early spring, when they started paying one of the older day students who had acquired his driving license to pick me up on his way to school and drive me home at the end of the day.

The school decided it was time for me to become a boarding student. (I found out years later that the faculty made a decision that it was safer for me to live on campus than to face a trip home at the end of the day in a car driven by a parent who was likely to have had a few gin and tonics before picking me up.) My father decided that if I were going to be a boarder, I may as well go to a school that he approved of: one that taught its students to call their teachers by their formal names, one with courses about military heroes, and one with an equestrian program. He knew of an all-girls school in Massachusetts that would be just the ticket for me. I didn't agree; I was happy at WCS.

But my father wanted to stick to his plan. In the late winter of my 9th grade year, he sent me the application forms for the horsey school. I dragged my feet about filling out the forms, and the application deadline approached. Finally, my father sent away for extra forms and filled out the application for me. He wrote a lively essay on the assigned topic, "If you could meet someone famous, dead or alive, who would it be, and why?" He had decided that I wanted to meet Ulysses S. Grant. "He was one of the strongest tacticians in the entire Civil War," he wrote on the first line. At the end of the essay, he signed my name. He gave me the form so I could answer one question he had not been able to tackle: "Who is your favorite teacher and why?"

I didn't answer that question, and the school's application deadline passed. My father called the school to see if I could have an extension but the place was already fully enrolled, so I moved into the girls' dorm at WCS the following September as a 10th grade boarding student. That year I met Lizzie, who became my best friend at school. She was tall, like me, and had black hair so long and straight that she could sit on it. All her clothes were black: black jeans, black T-shirts, black socks, black shoes. She had big, dark brown eyes that she rimmed with black eye shadow, and she applied white lipstick on her mouth to complete the ghoulish affect. My brother Teddy called her "Draculina."

Lizzie spent most of the day in the art studio. She owned her own pen set with different tips for thick and thin lines, and she stored her bottles of red, blue, black, and brown ink on a special shelf that belonged just to her. She drew elaborate portraits, elongating a nose here or enlarging some ears there, but you knew exactly who the person was. I thought she was terrific.

Lizzie and I were roommates in my junior and senior years. Every morning as soon as I got up and washed my face and brushed my teeth, I made my bed. Lizzie never made her bed. She just threw the covers into a heap near her pillow. I folded my clothes carefully in my bureau drawers, but Lizzie had her bureau moved out of her corner of the room so she had space for her drawing table. She kept her clothes in a cardboard box that had once housed a dishwasher, and she would move the box around if it got in the way. Every morning, she would rummage through the box to find a shirt or a pair of pants. At the end of the school year, it took me hours to pack my clothes neatly in suitcases and my records into padded boxes, so they wouldn't break on the way home. Lizzie just threw most of her possessions into the box, wrote her name on it in big letters, lugged the box up to the dorm's attic, and walked out with a backpack.

Lizzie and I complained a lot about the place, but we wouldn't have wanted to go to school anywhere else. My childhood friend Danny Perkins wasn't so lucky. He was sent to an all-boy's boarding school that his father, uncle, and two brothers had attended. He hated it there. For one thing, he didn't seem to fit in. Most students were competitive both in the classroom and on the athletic fields. But Danny was gentle and thought of himself as a musician and photographer. He played the flute and took pictures of leaves on the ground and the corners of his house in the afternoon light. I still have a series of photographs he took of me. He asked me to stand under a tree in his backyard and look off into the distance. My profile peers out from under a branch, heavy and full with leaves. Shadows cover my face.

Danny wore clothes that other students at his school considered weird. When he was 14, he decided that white was the most flattering color for him, so most of his wardrobe consisted of white painter pants with loops at the side, white T-shirts tucked into the waistband, white sneakers, and a white beret, pushed toward the side of his head. And he wore his hair long and hanging down so that it covered the edges of his face.

During his freshman year at his boarding school, he spent New Year's at our house. This was his first time in our town during the winter. We walked along the snow-covered road to the lake and built a snowman on our front lawn. On Saturday afternoon, as the light turned to gray and the shadows elongated into the snow, turning the world into a flat gray plate, Danny and I went sliding down the hill above our house. Before we took a second run, we paused at the top to catch our breaths.

Danny told me how lonely and miserable he was and how he wanted to transfer to my school or go to some school closer to his home. As he stood up and pointed the sled down the hill, he began to weep.

When I was 16 and a junior at WCS, I got up the courage to invite my school friend Luke home for dinner during a school vacation. Luke was also a boarding student, and he and I had been circling each other with increasing interest for weeks. Once, we had even held hands in the school's dining hall. He was spending the vacation with a friend who lived about a half hour away. He was a year older than I was, had a driving license, and could use his friend's car, so I had hoped we could spend some time together during the two weeks off from school. I was so excited that he was coming to my house for dinner.

My mother was away visiting friends, so Mrs. Deller had cooked dinner for us before she left. We were having one of my family's favorites: rare roast beef with Yorkshire pudding. I was afraid that my father would quote from some Frost poem or begin to recite some passages from Henry V. He didn't do either, much to my relief, but he did regale us with some of his war stories. He invited us to view the scar where a bullet had grazed his leg. We heard about that famous Army poker game. Then he moved on to horses. We listened to him talk about the grace of Thoroughbreds and the sturdiness of Morgan horses. He recited the names of some of the better-known stallions and steeplechase winners. Luke had done his homework and came prepared to talk about horses. He had learned that horses were measured in "hands" and he knew what a saddle girth was. He had been able to ask my father how many mares and geldings we owned. My father was impressed, and I was puffed up with pride.

My father moved on to speak about foxhunting. Foxhounds, in my father's opinion, were among the noblest of beasts. They were brave and fast, and they instinctively understood the thrill of the hunt. He was charming and hospitable in the beginning of his lecture, but as red wine helped him wash down some of his food, his mood took a darker turn.

He began to instruct us on the intricacies of the relationship between the riders and the hounds. "The Master of the Hunt," he said, turning his head sluggishly from Luke to me and back again, "calls to the hounds. With his horn, he can urge them forward or call them back." The communication he described was profound, spiritual. He chewed on some roast beef with his mouth half open and then left the table to get his fox horn that was hanging in a room at the back of our house where we kept our boots and coats. He returned and blew a short blast and a longer call to show his skill. He was Master of his own Hunt—Prince of the Hounds. The horn was attached to a leather strap around his neck. Pictures of foxes were etched around the horn's rim.

It was Luke's turn to respond. The evening had been going so well that he felt comfortable to ask a question out of genuine curiosity. "Can the dogs bark to give each other directions?" he asked.

My father was dumbstruck. He clutched his wine glass tightly in his right hand and his knuckles turned white. He turned his head slowly in Luke's direction. His mouth fell open; his lips turned down in deep disappointment. The features on his face became set in frozen place.

"First of all," he began, slowly pronouncing the words as if Luke were a half-wit, "they are hounds, not dogs." He emphasized "hounds" and "dogs" by raising his voice and pointing in Luke's direction. "And second of all," he went on, lifting and banging the wine glass on the table, spilling red drops onto his placemat, "foxhounds do not bark. They bay, they sing, but they do not bark."

He struggled to his feet, pushing the chair away from the table. Luke sneaked a look my way. Could I help him out of this predicament, I felt him ask. A few seconds passed. Even though we were only half-done with the meal, I thought maybe I could ask Luke to help me clear the table and the two of us could finish eating in the kitchen.

My father added the final blow to Luke before we could get up to leave the room. "You look smarter than you actually are," he slurred, and with that, he weaved indignantly off to bed, the fox horn still dangling from his neck.

In my senior year at the school, I sometimes rode in the school van into the nearby village of Woodstock, at the time one of the wealthiest communities in that area of the state, because it was full of people from New York and Connecticut who owned vacation homes there. My father's real estate office was located in a stately brick building near the town green. His business cards and brochures were stacked in the more expensive shops in town, and my parents had charge accounts around town. That meant that Lizzie and I could charge a snack at the diner, and I didn't have to spend my weekly allowance on shampoo.

Imagine my surprise one day in January when I walked into the drugstore to buy some toothpaste and was told I couldn't charge it. Word had spread around town that my family's bills were not being paid, and my father was spending more and more time at the bar in the stately inn at the other side of the green. Once when I dropped by on a Thursday afternoon to visit him, I found him snoring in his office chair, his head laying on the surface of his desk. At the end of February that year, a faculty member at WCS pulled me aside to tell me that my tuition bill hadn't been paid. "Unless this is taken care of in the next few weeks," he said, "You won't be allowed to return to school after spring break, so you'd better call your parents."

"That's ridiculous," my father said when I called home. "I'll take care of this."

Two days before two-week spring vacation began, my tuition bill still hadn't been paid, and I was told to pack up all my belongings. The next day the Headmaster drew me aside and told me not to worry about it; the problem had been solved. I found out years later that the school's Treasurer, who was wealthy and who often pumped money into the school's budget, had probably paid the outstanding balance on my tuition bill.

In early June that year, WCS held its annual dinner and dance for graduating seniors and their families. I had reserved seats for my parents in the dining hall, where small, hinged windows were high up on the wall. My parents did not show up for dinner. My table backed up against a corner behind a column, and as I sat through the meal with empty chairs on either side of me, I could see flies bumping up against the windowpanes.

The dance began at 7:00 p.m. and ended at 8:30 because in-dorm time was 9:00. My parents showed up at 8:15, reeking of alcohol. For the next fifteen minutes, they sashayed their way around the dance floor. WCS was an informal place, and teachers and students alike wore blue jeans and boots. My mother was wearing a floor-length, pale blue and white silk dress that flowed against her thin ankles.

My father was wearing his Hunt Ball outfit: a red tailcoat, a white bow tie, black dress trousers with a silk stripe down the outside of each leg, and black patent leather dancing pumps with matching satin bows over the toes. The shoes were old, the leather cracked, and the bows frayed.

The only dance step he could execute, even when sober, was a wooden box step. He wasn't sober, so his box step was off-kilter and off the beat. My mother wasn't sober either, but she was musical and could naturally move better, even when under the influence. She tried to make up for my father's clumsiness by flinging her legs around a little, making the skirt of her silk dress ebb and flow with her movements. After the two of them bumped into a few people on the dance floor, other dancers stayed clear of them, making them that more visible. I couldn't wait for them to go home.

The next morning at the end of breakfast, the Headmaster held up one of my father's dance pumps. "Does anyone know whose shoe this is?" he asked. "It was left on the dance floor last night."

Heads turned my way, and fellow students waited for me to make a sign. When I kept silent, so did they: acts of great kindness and solidarity, for which I remain grateful to this day.

Chapter 15
Moving Out

When my great-grandfather died, he left the property where I grew up to his children. Only one was interested in owning it—my maternal grandmother Margrette—so the other two sold out to her. When she died, she left it to her three living children: my mother, her sister Matilda, and her brother Ronald. The three of them decided that Aunt Matilda should own most of the property because she had married a rich Canadian and could afford the taxes and upkeep. My parents kept ownership of our house and yard (the original farmhouse) but had use of the entire property. In return, my mother and father were to take care of the property: keeping roads clear of snow in the winter, mowing the lawn at the edge of the lake in the summer, hiring a local farmer to hay the fields, and keeping an eye on houses that family members used only intermittently to be sure that pipes weren't leaking and the heat was running. In all practicality, we became managers of an estate that began to crumble as the years went by.

Still, this arrangement worked pretty well for a while. When we had to hire help, Aunt Matilda paid their salaries. She also paid the heat and water bills for the buildings (other than our own house) and the cost of keeping them up—like repairing roofs and repainting exterior doors and window trim. She and her family visited several times a year to enjoy the place, but finally she got fed up with the increasing costs of upkeep and taxes, and it was a long drive from where she lived—long enough to make weekend visits difficult. And she and her husband had bought a vacation property near where they lived in Canada, so their visits to Vermont trickled in number. Some years, they never showed up at all. My great-grandfather's house, the "Big House," had been unoccupied for nearly 10 years but was still being cleaned now and then and was being heated in the winter. My family and Uncle Ronald (who had returned and bought back his house from Matilda) and his family were the only permanent residents on the property.

Matilda tried to talk to my parents about selling off most of the property, but my mother would not even consider the idea. How could her sister ever mention such a blasphemy? The property was their home, where they entertained friends, swam in the lake, and rode their horses. And they worked so hard to keep the place up!

Matilda decided that if she were to continue paying most of the bills, she had to cut some corners. She tried to sell the "Big House," but no one was interested in owning it. It was time to tear it down. I was about ten at the time, but I remember my mother's hysteria when she saw the wrecking ball and all the dumpsters. My mother never forgave Matilda for this sacrilegious act. Their relationship moved from distant but warmly respectful to downright chilly.

Eight years later, during the summer before my first year in college, Aunt Matilda lost interest in continuing her involvement altogether and put the property she owned—which was most of it—on the market. A group of business people in town joined forces and agreed to buy the place, hoping to divide it into buildable lots for single families. My mother said at the time that she and my father found out about the sale only a few weeks before the Closing, but my cousin, Matilda's son, told me years later that my father had been a big help in putting the real-estate deal together. I'll bet he even earned a real-estate commission out of it.

Uncle Ronald would retain his house and an acre of land, and all that would be left for our branch of the family was our house and yard. We wouldn't be able to swim in the lake in the summer or play ice hockey on its frozen surface in the winter without permission, and my father and his friends couldn't ride their horses through the property. My parents decided to sell our house and to buy another house a few miles away, near a small village at the base of Mount Ascutney. They emptied out the old barn and filled a dumpster with the broken furniture pieces that they had been stacking until they got around to repairing them; the quilts with white stars that my mother never ended up using, moldy ski boots no one ever wore anymore, and the collections of rotting rope and rusty tools. They gave some of their older furniture in the house away, because now they would have four bedrooms instead of seven bedrooms; and the new house didn't have a sleeping porch.

It was a good thing, though, that the new property had a barn that was spacious enough for our horses and a brook that my parents dammed to create a pond where guests could swim in the summer and ice skate in the winter. An old friend gave them an abandoned maple sugar shack that was on his property. They had the shack moved to the pond's edge and added a chimney and woodstove at one end. Here people could sit and warm themselves in the fall and winter or stay dry during a light rain in the spring and summer. The yard at the side of the house was flat enough for the family croquet set, and there were some tall maples in front of the house that offered shade where people could sit on my great-grandfather's lawn chairs and watch others play the game.

The whole cycle started up all over again—weekend parties, a houseful of guests, flowing liquor. But my parents were older and their drinking was worse. One early morning while I was on home during a college break, I found my mother at the stove, preparing some casserole that she would freeze for their parties. There was a small glass of gin and ice nestled among the spices on the counter next to her. She still played bridge a few times a week, but then she'd drink so much sherry that she often wasn't able to cook dinner when she got home—even heating up a casserole was an effort. It was always a surprise to me that she made it safely home, since she was often driving under the influence.

One summer day when I was running some errands, using my father's car, I caught up with her as she was driving home from a bridge game. Her car was weaving all over the road. Luckily, traffic was light, which in our rural area meant that a car might appear every fifteen to twenty minutes. I passed her car and stopped in front of it (she was able to stop before she ran into me). A friend was with me, and she drove my father's car and I drove my mother's car. My mother passed out in the passenger seat a few minutes after we took off. As I rounded the last corner and headed up our driveway, she began to snore.

Another time she ran her car into a telephone pole at the end of the dirt road leading to our house; she nearly died of internal injuries. We all received a phone call from a doctor where she was hospitalized, telling us that if we wanted to see her again, we should visit her as soon as possible. She survived, though. Both my parents seemed to have nine lives.

These experiences did not stop her and my father from drinking, and he also began to drink more. Now and then, he would drink around the clock—awake for four hours, asleep for four hours, awake for four hours, asleep for four hours. Sober for none. But he was still the Commander of the family, trying to keep the new property up to his standards. The local farmer who had hayed the fields at the old property in the summer did the same thing at the new place. But now the man refused to help put the bales in our barn, because my father was supposed to help him, too—that was part of the original deal—and he was usually too drunk to lift any bales. When that happened, the man took his share of the hay bales and left the rest in a pile in front of the horse barn.

Then arrangements had to be made to move the bales into the hayloft. My father usually hired people for the day to help—teenage boys, home for the summer. But one summer afternoon it was about to rain, and the boys weren't supposed to show up until the following day. Wet hay bales can be a fire hazard because sometimes they combust. To avoid these problems, wet bales have to untied and the hay spread out in the sun to dry. It was therefore important that afternoon to get the bales into the barn before it started to rain. I couldn't move all the bales by myself, and my father was too inebriated to be of much help. He was still cognizant enough, though, to call a neighbor up the road: a young man named David—to tell him (not ask him) when to show up to help. David did not like being told what to do, so he wasn't about to jump up and rush down the hill to help stack hay bales, just because my father had issued the order.

Next, my father called Walter O'Day, the same man who used to sit in the heated mid-station at the ski area. Walter lived about a quarter of a mile down the road and by that time was quite elderly, but in the spirit of being a good neighbor, he came over to give what help he could. When David found out that Walter had been drafted, he felt forced to go down and join the crew, if for no other reason than to prevent poor Walter from having a heart attack. My father was there, waving his arms and slurring out commands. Put this bale here. That bale over there. He stood in the middle of the aisle, making it difficult for us to get by him with the hay. Walter was struggling along, dragging a bale now and then along the floor. David would meet him and hoist the bale up on top of the growing pile in the barn.

My mother was preparing a lobster dinner as a celebration and a way to thank us. White wine was chilling in the refrigerator, and she was heating up one of her vegetable casseroles. No one ever ate the meal. Walter was exhausted and went home before all the bales were in the barn. My father hobbled up to the house and went to bed. David and I finished the job, but he was so angry at being manipulated into helping that he was damned if he would eat lobster in my parents' house. And my mother knew that I am allergic to shellfish. She was the only person left to enjoy the meal, but she was too upset to eat.

I found her sitting in the living room, weeping. "I cooked such a lovely dinner," she said, "and no one would eat it. And your father was so upset that David is angry with him. What did he do wrong?" I knew it was hopeless to try to be reasonable, since she always defended my father, so I just sat there, and after a few minutes she held my hand. She and I had never been very physically demonstrative with each other, so I was grateful for this show of affection, even though it was motivated in part by alcohol and her own grief.

She stopped weeping for a second or two, took a deep breath, and swiveled her body in my direction. "Thank you for listening," she said. "I never liked you much when you were growing up, but I guess I was wrong."

Chapter 16
Finding My Mate

You already met my husband Jeff in earlier chapters, but now I'm going to tell you how we met.

On the mistaken assumption that I could get some relief from the drunken scenes at home, I chose to go to college in the Boston area rather than to the University of Vermont. But I was in denial—either location was only several hours away from home, and the alcohol trail followed me wherever I went. Our mother would call Emily or me and tell us that our father was "going through a rough patch," and one of us would drive to Vermont to find him nearly comatose. Or one of us would go for a visit, find my mother with a black eye, and take her to one of our houses for a few days or a week until things "quieted down" at home. Our brother Teddy escaped all this drama because he had relocated to the West Coast (smart move).

In my senior year, my college instituted the "6-week work term" in the winter (I always suspected that the impetus was to save money on heat for classroom buildings). I was tempted to go back to Vermont and ski for a month, but the possibility of living at home was a strong deterrent. I hoped to get a teaching job when I graduated, so I thought that if I could volunteer teach somewhere nearby, it would look good on my resume and I could still live in my dorm room.

I heard about a progressive boarding and day secondary school for grades 7 through 12. The school was located outside the city and offered non-paying teaching apprenticeships to college students. I was minoring in elementary education and wanted to be a 4th grade teacher, but I figured I'd look at the school anyway. I called and scheduled an interview. The school consisted of a quadrangle surrounded by stucco-sided buildings. When I arrived, students were in classes, so no one seemed around. It was a sunny, dry day in mid-December. Snow had not yet settled permanently on the ground, but a recent snow spat had left spots of sparkling ice here and there—mostly in the shade at the bases of trees.

I don't remember much of the conversation I had with the person who interviewed me, but I remember that he offered me a non-paying, month-long apprenticeship. I wasn't sure I was interested. The school was so similar to the high school I had attended that it seemed to me to be a step backwards in my life if I worked there, even if only for a month. And the students I would be working with were older than ones I was ultimately interested in teaching. I also remember thinking that despite the difficulties at home, I could probably go home for a few weeks of skiing and volunteer to work in the local library. I figured for a month I could stand it. I would be out most of the day, anyway, and with the use of one of my parents' cars, I could come and go as I pleased. I would get lots of exercise and spend extended time in my beloved Vermont, to which I intended to return after graduating from college.

I decided to let the school know my decision in a few days, though—to give the impression that I had thought about it before turning down this opportunity. I walked out of the building in which I was interviewed and stepped onto the quadrangle. At that very moment, my future husband Jeff walked out of the science building to my right. He was in his first year of teaching there and had just ended one of his chemistry classes. He was wearing leather pants, cowboy boots, a cowboy hat, a coat and tie, and sunglasses. He had a beard, and his curly dark hair fell nearly to his collar. As he stepped across the landing and down the building's steps, the sunlight fell onto his face.

I was hit by a thunderbolt at the sight of him. I decided then and there that I had to meet this man, so I turned around, returned to the room where I had been interviewed, and said I would be delighted to accept the offer of a month-long, non-paying apprenticeship—a step that changed the direction of my entire life, because I ended up spending 28 years working at that school.

My husband Jeff, when I first set eyes on him.

Jeff and I lived together for six months and decided the week before Christmas that we wanted to stay together and start a family, so we might as well get married.

"I'm going to ask your father for your hand," Jeff said. "I can speak to him when we go up for Christmas next week."

I was horrified. "You must be kidding," I said. "Never. I don't need his permission to make decisions about my life."

"No, no," he replied. "He'll be hurt if I don't do that."

I just wanted to tell them our news and be done with it, but it seemed important to Jeff to follow this male-to-male ritual, so I reluctantly gave in. We stopped on the drive to Vermont to buy a bottle of champagne that we hid in a snowbank outside the house so we could share a celebratory drink with the family. As we neared the front door, I was filled with dread.

My mother served one of the family favorites: roast lamb with mint jelly. My sister Emily and her husband were also there for dinner. My father went into the kitchen before dessert to have a snort of vodka, and Jeff followed him in. I could hear the two of them murmuring together in the kitchen. I sat at my place in the dining room, feeling flushed and wishing I could slink away to the guestroom upstairs.

Then I heard my father burst into tears. Oh, God. I just knew he was horrified by the entire prospect of Jeff, who, after all, had grown up in New York and had a New York accent—an accent my father often called grating to the ear. The fact that he himself had been born in New Jersey didn't seem to make him more tolerant. And Jeff was a teacher so didn't make much money. He wouldn't be asking my father to find some expensive property to buy in the area where we could live once we got married. And he knew nothing about horses and couldn't play tennis or skate. The fact that he had an Ivy League education would pale in comparison to all these deficiencies.

I just knew that this was the end of the plans that Jeff and I had to spend our lives together. No independent future for me. I would be alone or have to live with my parents for the rest of their days, taking people's coats as they arrived at the door, warming up and serving my mother's casseroles to guests, getting up early the day after a party to clean up the house. I was trapped.

Just as I was about to bolt from the room, my father came back into the dining room with Jeff following quietly behind. My father stood at his place at the head of the table and picked up his wine glass. Tears were streaming down his face. "What's the matter?" Emily asked. "What's happened?"

My father waved his arm dramatically, and some wine sloshed out onto his sleeve. "I wish to announce," he said, in a booming voice that we could have heard from outside the house, "that my daughter and Jeffrey are now engaged." Everyone clapped. I felt like crawling under the table.

Jeff told me afterwards that when he caught up with my father in the kitchen, he had tapped him on the shoulder and said, "Roger, I'd like to ask you something."

My father had turned around to face him. "You want to marry my daughter," he had said, and that is when he'd burst into tears.

Probably from relief. How mortifying is that?

He insisted on calling his mother with the glad tidings. He put me on the phone. Grandmother had her usual sharp retort to offer when she heard the news. "It's about time that he asked for your hand," she huffed. "He's had you from head to foot for MONTHS!"

Chapter 17

Wedding Deception

I wanted to get married in my parents' backyard, which sloped down to an open field. Beyond was a deep valley where the road wove between green hills. Small farms dotted the landscape, and Mt. Ascutney rose up in front of the house, casting a shadow late in the afternoon across the road. I hoped to have the ceremony in early June, when it would be warm and the mountain would be blossoming into green. My parents were delighted with the plan.

Jeff and I didn't want a large crowd—just family and close friends. By January 15, my father was calling me every few days to tell me he'd added names to the guest list: my mother's bridge pals, the undertaker's family I had lived with when in 7th grade, my father's friends from the Equestrian Club, and even some of his old pals from his days in the Cavalry. The wedding-guest list got longer and longer. For every name I was able to veto, two other names appeared to take its place. I imagined a wedding in which I would have to prop my father up if he tried to walk me down the aisle, and I would try to ignore the inebriated guests. After one afternoon call when my father was so drunk that he could hardly talk, I had a panic attack. "Let's just live together," I told Jeff. "We don't have to get married to start a family. Who cares? It's just a ceremony."

"That's ridiculous," he replied. "We'll just go and get married without the hoopla. We can get blood tests tomorrow."

I felt guilty to sneak off like that, but it was the only way I figured I could go through with it without having a nervous breakdown. The next morning we had our blood tests and bought two wedding rings off the rack. The minister of a church near our apartment agreed to marry us in his study at 6:00 p.m. on an evening later that week. We had already made plans to go out to dinner that night with two couples we knew, and on our way to the restaurant, we got married and our friends were our witnesses. The entire ceremony took 20 minutes: 15 minutes to find a parking spot and 5 minutes to say our vows. What a relief. The deed was done.

My father was disappointed, though, that he and my mother weren't going to host a big wedding and have a celebratory wedding reception at their home. After all, he had invited all these people, and my mother was already cooking and freezing casseroles for the event. He offered another option. "We'll give you a luncheon wedding reception up here in June," he said. "You'll get some wedding gifts. And your mother and I will give you something really special."

I am ashamed to say that we were seduced by the idea of all those presents, plus I was driven by guilt that we had gotten married without any family members there, so we agreed to the plan. We made a list of what we needed—a new toaster, a decent set of cooking pans, some tall water glasses, new flatware—and my parents sent the list to the invitees. About 75 people attended—members of Jeff's family (6 people), and many of my parents' friends. Uncle Sherman was there, Aunt Amanda and Uncle James, and my favorite, Aunt Charlotte. Even Grandmother attended, and she was 88. I was three months pregnant at the time. I didn't think I was showing, but when Jeff and I arrived, my grandmother said, "You're getting fat. Better go on a diet." After that, I felt obligated to tell everyone who spoke to me that Jeff and I had gotten married the previous January, in case anyone else guessed my sorry state.

My parents had spiffed up the house for the reception: the living room and downstairs bathroom had been repainted, and a landscaper had cleaned up the flowerbeds in front of the house. They also hired a professional photographer on hand to take pictures, some of which

I still have today. In one of them, Jeff and I are sitting under a tree, holding hands and staring at our feet. We look as if we had just received the death sentence.

The event followed the usual plan: tables set up on the lawn under the trees, and salmon and green salad for lunch. The day was unusually warm. The croquet set was up, and a few of the guests played listlessly while others sat on chairs to watch the game. White wine and beer were available at a bar set up in the barn, where people could help themselves. If anyone wanted something stiffer, vodka and scotch were lined up in the living room on a dry sink my father had found at a local antique shop. My father got drunk, lurched off to bed before the reception was over, and slept most of the afternoon. My mother held herself together just long enough to see the fresh-fruit dessert served, and then she joined him.

Not every guest had brought a gift, which was a disappointment. We were hoping to get quite a treasure trove but there was still a respectable pile. Jeff and I unwrapped the boxes the following morning. The only thing we received that was on our original list was a pair of cooking pots. What else did we get? Twelve casserole dishes, a crystal wine decanter, and a silver ice chest with prongs to lift the ice. We gave the decanter and ice chest to my parents. The best present we got was a card table—something we didn't think we needed but that we've used steadily for the past 40 plus years.

My parents' gifts were tucked into a small white envelope with our names scrawled on the front: a check for $1,000 and a gift "certificate" for a set of silver at Shreve, Crump and Low, which consisted of a small piece of paper torn from my parents' two-inch by three-inch telephone pad, on which my father had scrawled, "On us—a set of silver. You can charge it to my account." Unfortunately, his Shreve, Crump and Low account had been cancelled a few years before due to non-payment, and the $1,000 check bounced when we deposited it into our checking account, costing us $15 in bank fees.

Appearances meant a lot in my parents—lavish Christmases, huge parties, fancy cars, and charge accounts at places like Brooks Brothers and Shreve, Crump and Low. As long as we "kept up appearances," those unfortunate times when one parent or another passed out at the dining room table, when my mother showed up with a bruised lip or a black eye, or when a local vendor cancelled one of our charge accounts, didn't matter so much.

My parents liked to give lavish gifts that they could then brag about, like the $1,000 check for Jeff and me when we got married. When I graduated from college, my father said, "We'll send you $100 a month for a year, to help you get started." He told my grandmother about this gift, and she was proud that he had given me something so useful. Three months later, he called me up to rescind the gift. "I can't afford it," he said. "Sorry. But I have to pay the rent for my Mercedes, which I need for business."

When Jeff and I had our first child, they sent us a silver cup, engraved with "To our grandson, from his grandparents," with our son's birthdate underneath. I had no intention of ever letting our baby sip milk or any other kind of liquid from that cup, but out of respect for the thought behind the gift, I stuck the cup on the top shelf in the living room of our small apartment.

About two months later Jeff and I received a $75 invoice for the cup. I called my father. "What's up?" I asked. "I got this bill for the cup."

"Oh, just send it to me," he said. "That's a mistake."

The next month, I got a Statement, with "overdue" written on the bottom. "Oh, for God's sake," my father said. "I sent them a check last month."

Two more months passed, and then I got a letter from the store. "To avoid having this debt turned over to a collection agency," the letter stated, "please pay the bill or return the cup."

Coward that I am, I paid the bill.

Chapter 18
The Decline

When my parents were in their 80s, their situation became perilous, even by our standards, familiar as we three—my brother, sister and I—were to crisis after crisis.

The house they were living in was several miles from the village, and on snowy Vermont winter days, the people we hired to check on them every day and to cook meals for them couldn't reach their house, perched as it was on top of a hill and accessed by a dirt road. My father spent most of his days and nights in a relentless, alcohol-sodden fog. My mother had been suffering a series of strokes for several years and had finally lost her ability to speak, read, and write. Once when my husband and I arrived to visit them, we found the house full of smoke because they had a fire going in the fireplace and the chimney damper was closed.

Something had to be done.

Teddy, Emily, and I had a "summit meeting," and the three of us decided that we should try to move our parents into a smaller house located in a village with more people around to help care for them and to help us monitor the situation. We hoped that this would buy some time before we might be forced to consider an assisted living facility, if we could find one that would take them on. For years, our father had refused to consider a move. "You just want to ship me off to a nursing home," he frequently accused whenever one of us questioned their living situation. "I'll just go to the Veteran's Hospital. You can help me pack." Often I was tempted to say, "Good idea," but I never did.

The first step was to put their house on the market. "Their house" is a generous phrase. Legally the three of us owned the house, so we did not need their permission to sell the property. The deed had been transferred to our names when about five years earlier we had been called by the bank and been told that our parents weren't paying the mortgage payments and that the bank was about to foreclose. We had driven to Vermont to find shoeboxes of unpaid bills in my father's "office": an old sugarhouse in the backyard. At the time, a family friend who was an attorney set up a plan whereby the three of us would purchase the house, in return for which we would take out a mortgage in our names and pay off their mortgage and bills. Our parents would then give us a second mortgage for the rest of the house's value, and every year they would gift us a certain amount of the money due. Our parents could stay in the house under this plan, but Teddy, Emily, and I became even more enmeshed in their lives and the decisions they made or did not make but should have.

Even under this rescue plan, it had proven difficult to control our parents' spending habits. We'd show up for visits and find some "new" antique in the living room, or our father would tell us he'd just promised a donation to the local hospital or to the Equestrian Club. And the bills that our mother had accumulated from her earlier yearly trips to Florida when she could still speak kept increasing, as interest piled onto principal. In desperation, the three of us finally took control of their finances. I became recipient payee for our mother's social security check, so that the money would be spent on food and bills instead of on alcohol. Emily and Teddy took turns handling their checking account. We also agreed to contribute monthly to that account, since we now had control over it.

I had only been married for a few years at that time, and Jeff and I were raising a young family. Since Teddy and Emily were older, they were more financially stable than I was, and they were generous in letting me contribute a reduced amount. Still, I didn't think it fair that Jeff shoulder this expense, so I worked part-time while our children were in school, even though I had wanted to be a "stay-at-home Mom" while they were little. When I visited our parents and saw them consume expensive liquor and host dinner guests on money that we had given them, it was hard to bear. Often when I drove home from such visits (which became less and less frequent), I would yell and cry in frustration over the entire arrangement. And yet I felt trapped; if I pulled out, I would be the family pariah.

We put our father on a small allowance, but still he would call every few weeks and ask for more. He thought that they needed more firewood for the winter; he figured that the front porch needed to be repainted; the living room needed to be repainted; we should hire someone to go there three days a week rather than just one to do landscaping work. The requests escalated in demanding tone and expense.

It was time to tell our parents of our decision to sell the house and help them move to a smaller home that would be less expensive to maintain and to heat. We three went to Vermont so we could present a united front when we delivered the plan. We arrived at about the same time to find our father passed out on his chair in the study. One of his legs had fallen off a footstool and he was snoring, his mouth open and drooling. A half-empty bottle of Irish Whiskey and an empty glass were on the table in front of his chair alongside a small plate with cheese and crackers: an alcoholic's version of a "TV dinner." We found our mother upstairs, crying; she had a red splash across her cheek. Since she was not able to speak to us, she mimed with her arm and fist that our father had hit her in the face.

Teddy thumped downstairs and woke up our father. "How could you do that?" we heard him yell. "How could you hit her?"

"I did NOT!" our father responded in a booming voice, as if he were standing at a podium. "I would NEVER hit your mother." If the situation hadn't been so pathetic, we would have snickered. What does one do except throw the man out—a step we had never taken before and did not take in this situation, either. In hindsight, though, we probably should have done so, since in the end it came to that.

The next morning when things had settled down a bit, our father was coherent (it was early), and the swelling and redness on our mother's cheek had subsided. Before our family meeting, the phone rang. It was my husband Jeff. I had told him the night before about the scene at the house when we arrived. I said I couldn't speak then because we were just starting to discuss the move with our parents.

"What are you talking about?" he said. "Why isn't that man in jail?"

As the five of us sat down, the arrangement of chairs was unfortunate: our parents sat in straight-backed wooden chairs, facing the three of us scrunched onto a lower couch that was on the other side of the room. A fire was crackling in the fireplace; it was a beautiful fall day and the red leaves of maple trees outside the house were shimmering in the morning sun.

As we began to talk, our mother sat in her chair and looked at the three of us without any facial expressions crossing over her face. She was so diminished by strokes that the haughty temper that she had so often displayed when she was younger and was told to do something she didn't want to do was by then muted. Our father, on the other hand, was surprisingly cooperative. We should have been wary but were so relieved that we were seduced. "This makes sense," he said. "This is a pretty big house for the two of us. I'll ask the real estate agent I brought into the business to work with us on pricing and marketing." He paused and then added, "But we'll have to do some sprucing up first, such as fixing the barn and replacing the heating system."

The three of us sagged into our chairs and glanced at each other. Finally, Emily came to our rescue. "Let's see what the agent says," she replied. "We may not have to take these steps."

Our father called us several days later and said that the real estate broker had recommended an asking price of over a million dollar. "Such a lovely piece of property," he said. "She recognizes its worth." Well, not many other people seemed to agree, because the property sat on the market for four or five months without a viewing. We finally asked the real estate agent to meet with us directly. She admitted that our father had set this asking price and that she had felt at the time that the price was much too high and had told him so. Looking back now, through the span of years since our parents died, it seems surprising that we were so duped, but we had had a lifetime of being taught to submit to our father's authority, and we had learned the lesson well.

The situation between our parents became even more worrisome, if that's possible. More often than not, we would hear from people we had hired who helped our mother get dressed and bathe that she had bruises on her torso. And when we called our parents, our father was sometimes incoherent and by that time, our mother had lost the ability to speak. We were worried and decided that the two of them should be separated. Instead of getting rid of our father, however, we moved our mother out of the house and set her up in Emily's vacation home, a few miles up the road. A full-time helper lived with her, and our father was able to visit her now and then when the helper would go and pick him up. We were comforted by the fact that there was someone living with her all the time, so that our parents would never be alone together.

We lowered the asking price for the house, and people began to come to view the property, but our father did not seem to cooperate with the marketing plan. Sometimes, when the agent called to set up a viewing, he would say he was busy and they would have to choose another day. Or the agent and perspective buyers would show up and he would try to take control of the appointment, offering to give the visitors a tour or asking if they would like a whiskey, even in the morning. Sometimes when the real estate agent arrived after lunch with prospective buyers in tow, our father would be drunk. Once he had passed out on the floor and his body blocked the front door. We realized that if we were ever to get the property sold, he would have to leave. We did not know where he would go, but we were desperate, and Emily gave him the bad news.

He didn't go far. He moved into a new resort a few miles away, where he had his own one-bedroom apartment with a kitchenette and fireplace. He could walk to the village store for supplies and visit the bar in the main building of the resort. He had traded the big drafty Colonial where he was all alone for a cozy little apartment with room service and a ready supply of alcohol. And who was paying for all this? His mistress, whom I mentioned earlier and whom you will meet in the next chapter.

The house finally sold and we moved our parents to a nearby village, closer to where some of the people who took care of them lived. The house was pleasant with three bedrooms, a large living room with a fireplace, a nearby barn, and a spacious backyard. When the windows were open, you could hear the soothing sound of running water in a brook down the street. In many ways, the house was a smaller version of the house they had been living in. It was also larger than the condominium that my husband and I and our two young children were living in at the time.

Our mother didn't like the house; the property was beneath her. She would scrunch up her face and look as if she had just eaten a lemon whenever we asked her how she liked her new home. She spent most of the day sitting on the couch watching television. Our father seemed content, though. His drinking was uninterrupted, and he made friends with a few of the men in the neighborhood who would stop by now and then for a free drink. He could walk to the village store for wine and to the village library to borrow books that he read late into the night between drinking bouts. He joined a reading group at the local library but unfortunately, the group met in the evening, when he had difficulty even making it up the stairs to his bedroom. Walking to the library down the street and participating in a coherent conversation would have been tough.

A childhood friend of Teddy's who worked at a local ski area spent several winters living in the house: an advantage for him since he didn't pay for room and board, but he was also company for our father and an able body in case they needed help. Now and then a visiting nurse stopped by to check on our mother. Emily was a constant in our parents' lives during the summer, when she and her family were ensconced in their nearby vacation home. Now and then Teddy would drive down from northern Vermont where he had moved after his time in California, but several years later he retired and moved to South Carolina and his visits ended. I didn't see our parents very often because I found it so painful, but one September I caved into my father's invitations and went up to Vermont for a visit.

I took our daughter with me. Our son was in college at the time but our daughter was still in high school. She was worried that my mother wouldn't last much longer, so she wanted to go with me.

I was apprehensive about what we would find when we arrived, but I didn't feel as if I had the right to deny her request. Still, I planned a short visit; we would only stay in their guest room for one night.

We arrived at the house in the late afternoon. My father was sitting in his chair by the fire with a glass of scotch in his hand; my mother was slumped down on the couch. No plans had been made for dinner, so I warmed up some leftovers that they had in the refrigerator. After we ate and I was in the kitchen washing dishes, I saw my father grab our daughter by the arm and lead her into a corner of the kitchen. "Your mother is impossible," I heard him slur as he pointed at me. "She's so difficult and rarely does what I ask. I hope you won't end up like her." Our daughter looked over at me beseechingly, and at that moment I had an epiphany.

This is it, I thought to myself. *I can't allow this kind of behavior to roll over to my children.* Our Caravan was large enough to sleep in. I grabbed our things, and our daughter and I headed to the car. I drove it to a nearby park, put the back seats down, and made a nest for us in the back. We had a peaceful night, and early the following morning I drove home with our daughter still soundly asleep in the back. I didn't see my parents again for two years. This was the last time our daughter saw her grandfather alive. At least she'd had that chance; our son didn't see his grandparents for nearly three years before they both died. I didn't encourage our children to visit; the chain of abuse and dysfunction had to be broken. I had finally drawn the line as far as my own family was concerned.

But once both our children were in college, Emily encouraged me to visit our parents. "They may not live much longer," she said, "and you will regret it if you don't see them." It was near my father's birthday and right after my own. He had always liked to couple his birthday and my own into one event. I discovered why after he died, which I will explain later.

I decided to stay in their house for only one night, and I brought with me a small birthday gift for him. I arrived in the late afternoon. My father had bought a small birthday cake for us to share, but he slept most of the afternoon in his chair during my visit. My mother looked depleted and exhausted. She was also incontinent; in the morning there was a stream of urine and feces from her first-floor bedroom into the bathroom. A nurse's aide was there to clean her up and get her and my father breakfast. I left shortly after I woke up, and I never saw the two of them together again. Three days later, my father died. My gift was still on his bureau, still wrapped.

Chapter 19
The End

A few days after I saw him for the last time, my father fell down the stairs in a drunken stupor and broke his neck, dying in less than a minute. He had just turned 86 the week before. His head lay on the threadbare Oriental rug at the foot of the stairs, around the corner from where my mother was sitting on the couch. One of her helpers was in the house at the time, cooking dinner. The woman told us later that she just figured that my father had passed out. It was only after she served my mother dinner that she realized that he was dead.

The woman reached my sister Emily by phone and she reached me at the school where I worked (I was running an evening meeting for parents). Emily and I drove to Vermont and arrived after our father's body had been removed from the house. Our mother was sitting on the couch and seemed to be in a fog. We put her to bed and tried to get some sleep ourselves. In the middle of the night we woke up to a freezing house. Their oil tank was empty; our father had not arranged for a fuel delivery. For the rest of the night I lit a fire in their fireplace and slept on the couch, getting up every few hours to keep the fire going. In the morning, we ordered an oil delivery and were required to pay for it in advance. Teddy was on a bicycling trip on the West Coast that he had planned for a long time, but we tracked him down and he flew to Vermont.

He arrived two days later. We weren't sure that our mother knew that our father had died, since she couldn't talk and seemed nonplussed, but when Teddy entered the house, she gave him our father's pipe and tobacco holder and gestured that he should sit in our father's chair by the fireplace. And she cried. We realized then that she knew what had happened.

During the following week after my father's death, Teddy, Emily, and I went over their things to clear out our father's possessions. We found that in addition to his clothing, much of which was shabby ("old but good quality"), our father had left his family eighteen dollars in his wallet and an unopened package of Brooks Brothers' underwear.

The three of us had breakfast together every morning and formed our "to do" lists for the day. Then we attacked the tasks on our individual list: calling our parents' friends to tell them the news, writing the obituary, organizing a memorial service, sending death announcements and the date and time of the memorial service to local papers, meeting with our parents' lawyer and helping to care for our mother. We asked her if she wanted to attend the memorial service, and she shook her head "no."

We agreed that we should tell our father's mistress of his death. After all, she was like his second wife, and they were parents together. "Are you having a service?" she asked after we gave her the sorry news. "May I attend?" The three of us agreed to let her come, since our mother wouldn't be there. It was my job to pick her up from the airport and drive her to a local hotel. During our drive together, I found out that her birthday was the same day as mine, robbing me of the thought that my father chose to celebrate his birthday with mine because he wanted to share something special with me.

We held the memorial service a few days later in a local community church that doubled as a small theater. My father's second cousin Stuart, a minister, officiated. We had no idea how many people would attend and were astonished when over 40 people showed up—some of them wearing riding outfits, as if ready for a foxhunt to honor my father's memory.

It was a Quaker-like service, similar to the one we had held for GRANDmother eight years before. Each of us—children and grandchildren—stood at the front of the space and shared memories and tributes. While working on this book I found the statement that I composed over 25 years ago to read at the service. I spoke about my father's many playful qualities, but I also spoke about his complexities. "I will work hard in the years ahead," I wrote, "to remember his gifts and strengths, so that they will outshine the hard times and the struggles."

After each of us had had a chance to say something, we opened up the floor to anyone else who would like to contribute. A few people stood and shared experiences they'd had with our father at horse shows when he was a judge. One woman who had worked at the local prison told the story about the time she had checked our father in to serve his 7-month DUI stint "in the jug." "Most of the prisoners showed up with their possessions in paper bags," she said. "He was the only one who showed up with a Gucci suitcase." Several people chuckled.

Stuart asked if anyone else would like to speak. After a moment of silence Stuart cleared his throat as if to close the service, when our father's mistress stood up. No one in the room knew who she was except for Teddy, Emily, and me. She cleared her throat before she began to read from a piece of paper she held in her hand. "What words can I speak here for Roger?" she began, pausing at the end of the question for dramatic effect and looking out over her audience. We could hear the shifting of bodies in the wooden pews as people turned in her direction. It was a long poem, so I am quoting only a few lines here:

> "What can I say of that brave mythical head?
> All the words spoken and all left unsaid...
> But still I grieve for him
> And taste the salt of tears."

She read in a strong and dramatic voice. You could have heard a pin drop in the church. People turned their heads in disbelief to look at us, still standing at the front of the church. Who was this woman?

The poem ended with:

> "Pray for his soul, lay him to rest,
> One of the loveliest,
> One of the best."

As she sat down, silence filled the church. She had made quite an impression, even though at the time I wished she had just sat quietly and not drawn attention to herself. *She probably practiced reading that in front of a mirror,* I thought to myself. We all murmured the Lord's Prayer in closing and then many people fled the church. A few people who were old family friends stayed for the reception we held in the rooms beneath the sanctuary. My father's mistress caught a ride back to her hotel a few minutes after leaving the church. We heard afterwards that she had arranged to have a driver take her to the airport for her flight home. At the reception, some people asked us who she was, but most people avoided the subject.

Our parents had loved lilacs and had several large lilac bushes around their house. Our father used to pick the blossoms and put them into vases for the living room and dining room. In our father's will, he had requested that he be cremated and his ashes spread into the brook behind the big Colonial where they used to live. He also directed that someone play the bagpipes at the same time. We paid for the cremation but the rest was not possible to arrange. First, we didn't know anyone who could play the bagpipes. And second, we weren't comfortable with spreading his ashes into a brook that was now on someone else's property. So Emily, Teddy, and I had decided to spread his ashes in the field behind Emily's vacation home and also to bury some at the base of a lilac tree in her backyard.

In the days that followed the service, Teddy resumed his bicycle trip, and Emily and I tried to find someone to live with my mother until and after her health improved. We were unsuccessful in doing so, and our mother's doctor told us that our mother should be in a nursing home for a while so she could receive the medical care that she needed. In the hope that she would recover some of her strength, Emily and I set about trying to find a nursing home or an assisted living facility near where both of us lived in Massachusetts (by then Teddy had returned to his home in the South).

We visited several nursing homes and assisted living facilities that smelled like hospitals. One of them had a community room where people sat in wheelchairs, silently watching TV. One woman was tied into her chair so she wouldn't flop over. In another nursing home, we passed a room where a nurse was helping a very old woman into bed. The woman's face seemed colorless and was full of wrinkles and folds, but her eyes were bright and aware, and she looked out into the hallway at us with a sharp youthfulness that I found disconcerting.

We finally found an assisted living facility that seemed okay—it was a small facility, consisting of several older buildings that used to be private residences. Caregivers wore regular clothes, and people who lived there were free to walk around the grounds. But the place wouldn't even consider accepting our mother while she needed so much nursing care.

Instead of getting better, our mother got sicker and sicker and clearly was not ready to move out of the nursing home. Emily and I took turns checking on her. We were lucky to find a buyer for our parents' house, and now we had the funds to pay for a private room for her in the nursing home. The day she was moved into the private room, Emily and I brought in some plants and flowers to cheer the place up. One of Emily's sons was there. My husband Jeff arrived mid-morning from Massachusetts with our daughter; her college was located on the way to Vermont, and she had wanted to come (our son was in college a further distance away). We all hung family pictures over our mother's bed, and our daughter sat on her bed and held her hand.

My mother had another stroke the weekend before Thanksgiving. The nurses taking care of her warned us that she was near the end, but she seemed to rally, as she always had in the seven or eight years since she'd had her original stroke. I drove up to see her on Sunday and was encouraged. She was able to walk, though with a limp, and knew me and seemed aware of what I was saying. She was eating well, too. I went home that afternoon feeling reassured. On Tuesday, Emily drove up from Massachusetts to spend Thanksgiving at her vacation house with her family, as she did every year. She called me at work Tuesday afternoon. "You'd better come up," she said. "She doesn't look good." Teddy flew up, too, and we all stayed at my sister's house. Since we were not sure how long our mother would live, my husband Jeff stayed in Massachusetts to receive our children home from college for the long Thanksgiving weekend.

On Wednesday morning, my mother stopped eating and lay passively in bed. When we entered the room, her eyes turned in our direction, but she drew her hands away when we tried to touch them. On Thursday, Thanksgiving Day, Emily and I sat in her room playing Scrabble on a card table we had brought with us and eating turkey sandwiches. My mother woke up once but refused our offer of water, clamping her jaws tight and holding her lips close.

By Friday, she seemed a corpse, as if her spirit were gone and all that was left was for her heart to stop beating. Her skin seemed colorless, her lips were drawn back from her teeth, and her breath was uneven. We watched as four or five seconds went by without her seeming to inhale, then a ragged intake and her chest rose. Her hands were cold when I touched them. She died around dawn on Sunday—eight weeks and two days after my father's death. She was 85 years old.

She had also requested that her body be cremated, so we had the luxury of holding her memorial service in June: her birth month and her favorite time of year. That gave us time to recover from the whirlwind of the last eight and a half weeks that had passed since our father's death. It also gave us time to compose a formal announcement of the service and send it to our parents' surviving friends. We chose Robert Frost's poem "A Prayer in Spring" as the centerpiece of the announcement, because the poem seemed to capture our mother's love of sunlight and flowers and the way she always seemed to enjoy the moments in front of her when she was with her friends and family.

> "Oh, give us pleasure in the flowers today:
> And give us not to think so far away
> As the uncertain harvest; keep us here
> All simply in the springing of the year.
>
> Oh, give us pleasure in the orchard white,
> Like nothing else by day, like ghosts at night;
> And make us happy in the happy bees,
> The swarm dilating round the perfect trees.

And make us happy in the darting bird
That suddenly above the bees is heard,
The meteor that thrusts in with needle bill,
And off a blossom in mid-air stands still.

For this is love and nothing else is love,
The which it is reserved for God above
To sanctify to what far ends He will,
But which it only needs that we fulfill."

It was a beautiful early-June day in Vermont, with a slight breeze that rustled through the newly born leaves—the kind of day when our mother would be sitting on her patio in one of her florid bathing suits, soaking up the sun. The kind of morning when she would be making sandwiches and packing the gin and tonics for her picnic lunch at the lake with her best friend Mrs. Borderly, who by then was long deceased.

As we had at our father's memorial service, we decided that as a family, each of us would choose something to say in her memory— something we had written or something published that had special meaning for us and seemed right for the person she was. As I prepared my statement for her service, I felt again that rising panic in the face of my parents' alcoholism and the violence between them—and remembered afresh how out-of-control everything often seemed in my childhood house.

I grieved my parents' loss, but I also felt enormous relief. No more calls in the middle of the night to tell us that Dad had fallen down drunk. No more visits to find my mother with a bruise on her cheek. No more bill collectors repeatedly calling and threatening. No more friends telling us how elegant and charming our parents were. No more hiding, lying, and living a secret life that wasn't much of a secret to our neighbors and to other people who knew us.

Over twenty-five years have passed since my parents died, and I am now nearly as old as they were when they died. As I've aged, my childhood experiences stand out more clearly in my mind. The smell of lilacs reminds me of the vases in our house, full of freshly picked blossoms from the lilac tree outside our front door. The summer sun warming my back as I walk across our yard transports me to the jaunts I used to take across the fields of my childhood, my Flippity

Flop by my side. I remember my mother taking me with her when she gathered unfurled fiddlehead ferns at the shaded edges of the woods near our house, and when the two of us weeded her flower and vegetable gardens and made applesauce by boiling apples that grew on a wild apple tree behind our yard. When my eyes water as I chop onions, I am transported back to when I helped my mother make her endless casseroles, to be frozen for yet unscheduled parties.

I remember when my father took me out of school on the first day of fishing season almost every year, so the two of us could go fishing together in trout streams near our house, and how he taught me to take a fish off a hook in a way that would do minimal damage if a fish was too small to keep. Then I would throw it back into the water and hope that it would live. And those great, family poker games when we laughed together and felt the thrill of winning.

I have come to appreciate more and more the positive gifts my parents gave me: to relish friendships, to be a committed part of a group, and to laugh in the moments of life, whether those moments are grim or joyful. In death, my parents are finally sober together, and I am able to remember them without so much fear and anger and to think of them in a more loving way. And at last, at last… I have begun to accept and to forgive myself.

Sources

1   Twerski, Abraham J. "Most children of alcoholics…" https://www.goodreads.com/author/quotes/64641.Abraham_J_Twerski

2   Williams, Robin. "An alcoholic is someone who…" https://quotefancy.com/quote/2664883/Robin-Williams-An-alcoholic-is-someone-who-can-violate-his-standards-faster-than-he-can

3   Eliot, T.S. "Only those who will risk…" https://www.brainyquote.com/quotes/t_s_eliot_161678

4   Gerritsen, Tess. "The Christmas tree, twinkling…" https://quotefancy.com/quote/1528824/Tess-Gerritsen-The-Christmas-tree-twinkling-with-lights-had-a-mountain-of-gifts-piled-up

Family Members and Friends

My family members, relatives, and my family's friends and neighbors:

My husband: Jeff

My birth family:

Father: Roger
Mother: Helen
Brother: Theodore (Teddy)
Sister: Emmeline (Emily)

Relatives on my father's side:

Grace: My paternal grandmother
Frank: My paternal grandfather
Cathy: My father's first cousin
Stuart: My father's second cousin

Relatives on my mother's side:

Frank Artemis Kennedy (FAK): My maternal great-grandfather
Margrette Kennedy Snow: My maternal grandmother
Sydney Snow: My maternal grandfather
Ronald: My mother's brother

Anne: Uncle Ronald's second wife
Matilda: My mother's sister
Aunt Charlotte: My mother's first cousin
Uncle Sherman: My mother's second cousin

My childhood friends and classmates:

Hannah Brown: My best friend in elementary school
Danny Perkins: My special summer friend
Willy Whittier: A classmate when I was in 7th grade

My high school friends:

Lizzie: My best friend
Luke: Another of my classmates

People who drifted in and out of our home and lives:

Mrs. Deller: My mother's housekeeper
Ms. Borderly: My mother's best friend
Samuel: A local lawyer
Nathaniel (Nate): Samuel's son
James and Amanda: A married couple
Beetle: Had an affair with Amanda
Betsy: Amanda's sister who had an affair with my father
Beverly: Had an affair with my father

People who lived in or near the town or village where my parents lived:

Henry Larkin: Local handyman
Mr. and Mrs. Fortune: Owned local, small supermarket
Sarah Talbot: The town's matriarch who held open houses at Christmas
Mr. and Mrs. Morrison: Local undertakers
Bates family: Local equestrian family
Walter O'Day: A local farmer

Author Bio

Connie and her husband Jeff split their time between Massachusetts and Vermont. She is a retired high school English teacher and is co-author of five published, non-fiction books on indoor air quality and a six-book educational series on expository and creative writing for middle-school students.